PENTECOST
AND
AFTER

Studies in the Book of Acts

Books by M. R. De Haan

M. R. De Haan Classic Library

PENTECOST AND AFTER

Studies in the Book of Acts

M. R. DE HAAN

Grand Rapids, MI 49501

Library of Congress Cataloging-in-Publication Data
De Haan, M. R. (Martin Ralph), 1891–1964.
  Pentecost and after: studies in the book of Acts / M. R. De Haan.
      p.   cm. (M. R. De Haan classic library)
  Originally published: Grand Rapids, Mich.: Zondervan Publishing House, 1964.
    1. Bible. N.T. Acts—Criticism, interpretation, etc.
I. Title. II. Series: De Haan, M. R. (Martin Ralph), 1891–1964). M. R. De Haan classic library.
BS2625.2.D4   1996   226.6'06—dc20   96-10337
                                                 CIP

ISBN 0-8254-2482-8

2 3 4 5 6 7 / 07 06 05 04 03

Printed in the United States of America

Contents

Foreword

"Of making many books there is no end; and much study is a weariness of the flesh" (Ecclesiastes 12:12). The purpose of this volume on *Pentecost and After* is not merely a matter of adding *another* book to the many already written. It is written because we were fully persuaded that it met a definite need at this particular time. Many other subjects and titles for another book came to mind, but we could think of none more timely than this new volume. There must always be a good reason for writing a book, and we give the following reasons (not excuses) for this latest addition:

1. We believe there is a need for this volume because of its timeliness. In recent years there has been a great revival of interest in the Bible teaching concerning the ministry of the Holy Spirit, and especially His manifestation on the day of Pentecost. However, the new emphasis on the doctrine has resulted in greater confusion and difference of opinions among evangelicals than ever before. It has not resulted in uniting believers, but rather it has promoted division of interpretations instead.

2. Because of the great emphasis placed on the ministry of the Holy Spirit in certain quarters, it has become the source of greater controversy. Never before have there been such wide differences among evangelicals in regard to the meaning of Pentecost. Never before has there been such confusion of tongues and conflicting opinions. This alone we felt called for a re-study and re-evaluation of the subject. Certainly the Holy Spirit is not the author of confusion, and the wide and numerous conflicting interpretations are proof-positive that the Holy Spirit is not the cause of this confusion. The cause must lie with those who have missed the one and only correct interpretation.

3. Because of these differences we have waxed bold enough in this volume to set down what we sincerely believe to be the truth. We do not claim infallibility, nor do we have our minds closed to added light. Nor do we want to impose our

views upon those who differ, but rather hope that our differences may lead to a re-study of the subject. We do not want to *encourage controversy* but rather *discussion*. If what we say promotes a closer study of the Word to see if these things are so, then it will be profitable — whether we agree or not. Any searching of the Scriptures, even if only for the purpose of bolstering our own views, or disproving another's will result in some measure of blessing.

Jesus said, "By their fruits ye shall know them." If in contending for our position, it makes us contentious, cantankerous, condemnatory and caustic, it is proof that it is not the work of the Holy Spirit at all. The fruit of the Spirit is love, joy and peace. If our experience gives us a sense of joy but lacks love, it is a false joy. And to claim we have peace without love, is only a pious fraud. With a prayer that this volume may help us to respect the honest convictions of other brethren, so that we may contend for our own convictions without becoming contentious, disagree without becoming disagreeable, and positive without becoming preemptory, we send forth this volume. "Let brotherly love continue" (Hebrews 13:1).

Preface

This volume *Pentecost and After* is based upon the book of Acts, but is definitely not an attempt to produce an exposition of the book as such. Certain portions of the book of Acts are passed over rapidly, some without any comment whatsoever. The rather, we pay attention to the most important portions or "high peaks." These mountain peaks are such chapters as Acts 2, 7, 10, 13 and 15. The aim of these chapters is to convey an over-all picture of the plan of the book in its totality.

The key verse is Acts 1:8. In this verse we have not only the outline of the book, but also the program for the present dispensation of the Church. It is the Lord's last commission, beginning at Jerusalem, Samaria, and the uttermost part of the earth. It begins with the Jew, then the half-Jew and half-Gentile Samaritans, and concludes with the Gentile.. It is the transition from the old covenant to the new, from law to grace, from the Kingdom to the Church. The first stage (Jerusalem) occupies chapters 1 through 7. Peter is the central figure. The second stage is introduced in chapter 8, and the central figure is Philip and the place is Samaria. The third stage begins with chapter 13 and the central figure is Paul and the scene revolves around Antioch. The book opens in Jerusalem and ends in Rome.

One more thing should be borne in mind. The first half of Acts contains the doctrine of Pentecost; the latter half, the history of Pentecost. The first part in Jerusalem and Samaria contains the great doctrines of the Early Church, while the last half contains the historical account of the carrying out of the purpose of Pentecost.

We repeat — this volume is occupied primarily with the first half of the book of Acts. It is not meant to be an exhaustive or verse-by-verse exposition, but rather an attempt to give the general character of the book built upon the high points and mountain peaks of the book. Great portions are passed over with only slight comment because they are an elaboration of the main and most important events in the book.

Finally, we must remember that Acts is a record of the transition from the Kingdom to the Church, from Judaism to Christianity. The legal Judaistic approach at Pentecost gradually gives way to the message of pure grace under the preaching of Paul. To apply everything in the book of Acts as a literal pattern for the Church today can only lead to confusion of tongues and deeper differences of interpretation. Unless we respect the *dispensational* character of Acts, we shall not be able to *rightly divide the word of truth.*

CHAPTER ONE

The Savior's Last Farewell

The Acts of the Apostles is the accepted title of the fifth book in order of the twenty-seven books of the New Testament. This place between the four gospel records and the epistles, while not the chronological order in which it was written, is certainly the logical order; and we cannot help but believe the compilers of the New Testament were divinely guided in placing the book of Acts between the gospels and the epistles, for it is the connecting link between the two. The book of Acts records the transition from Judaism to Christianity, from law to grace and from the Kingdom to the Church, the Body of Christ. Failure to distinguish between the program in the gospels and the program in the epistles is at the root of almost all the confusion among evangelicals, and the cause of the wide difference between the various groups of Bible-believing Christians. We earnestly believe that a correct interpretation of the book of Acts, and especially the meaning of Pentecost, would solve much of the confusion among believers concerning the ministry of the Holy Spirit in this dispensation. Unless we learn to "rightly divide" the Word and understand the true meaning and significance of Pentecost and its results, nothing but a conflict of opinions can result.

PENTECOSTALISM

The rapid recent spread of Pentecostalism with its countless shades and degrees of interpretation is in itself an argument for a careful re-examination of the book of Acts, Pentecost and the early history of the Church. The spread of this growing movement reveals a hunger for a better understanding of a truth which has been too sadly neglected. Because the organized church has failed to understand and teach the true place of the record of Acts, sincere Christians have turned to these Pentecostal movements in a desire to satisfy their hunger. To be sure, in many cases it was a jumping from the frying pan into the fire; and in an effort to get away from the cold mechanical dogmatic stagnation of formal religion they have gone over to the other extreme of another error. Because of the lack of fire in their churches, many true believers have fallen into the error of "wild-fire" instead. At least there was fire. We believe the extremes to which some of these reactionary movements have gone is due to a lack of understanding of the real place and meaning of Pentecost. This is our reason for taking up at this time the exposition of the book of Acts in these messages. They are not given in a spirit of condemnation, but in an honest attempt to arrive at the truth and clarify some misunderstandings. We do not judge anyone's sincerity, but simply wish to help the thousands who are seeking for truth, who are confused by all the conflicting testimonies and claims of the almost numberless groups springing up in these last days.

DIFFERENT OPINIONS

This very fact that there is so much difference of opinion among the promoters of the Holiness movements, indicates the need for clarification. The various names indicate this fact, for the champions of the movement are known by scores of names, such as: Pentecostal, Apostolic, Second Blessing, Holy Spirit Baptism, Latter Day Rains, etc., etc. It is self-evident that all cannot be right when there are so many differences. In our study of the book of Acts we shall seek to be guided not by feelings or emotions or personal evidences or traditions, but, as God gives us grace, by the simple Word of God, illumined by the Holy Spirit. We do not wish to offend anyone and we shall studiously try to avoid doing so. However, if the Word offends you, we cannot be held responsible.

THE AUTHOR OF ACTS

We begin the study of the book of Acts itself by calling your attention to the writer of the book. It is clearly indicated in the opening verses:

> The former treatise have I made, O Theophilus, of all that
> Jesus began both to do and teach,
> Until the day in which he was taken up, after that he
> through the Holy Ghost had given commandments unto the
> apostles whom he had chosen (Acts 1:1, 2).

From this brief introduction we learn that the writer of Acts
was Dr. Luke, who also wrote the third gospel. In the gospel
through Luke we read in Luke 1:3 that Dr. Luke wrote this
record presumably as a letter to a certain Theophilus. He says:

> It seemed good to me . . . to write unto thee . . . most ex-
> cellent Theophilus,
> That thou mightest know the certainty of those things
> wherein thou hast been instructed (Luke 1:3, 4).

Since the gospel through Luke was written to Theophilus, it
also immediately identifies Luke as the writer of Acts. The opening verse refers to the gospel through Luke when he says:

> The former treatise have I made, O Theophilus . . .
> (Acts 1:1).

The book of Acts, like the gospel, was apparently written
for the information of Luke's friend Theophilus. The name
"Theophilus" means "beloved of God." Besides this we know
little or nothing about this friend of Dr. Luke.

Acts then is a continuation of the gospel through Luke. It
takes up the story where Luke 24 ends. In the gospel through
Luke we have the record of the things Jesus *"began* both to do
and teach" (Acts 1:1) while here upon the earth *until* he was
taken into Heaven.

It is important to remember that the book of Acts is a continuation of Luke, and records the things Jesus continued to *do*
and to *teach* from Heaven, through the Holy Spirit. In Luke
we have Jesus' ministry *on earth;* in Acts we have a continuation of His ministry *in heaven,* through the ministry of the
Holy Spirit. Some have therefore suggested that the name
"Acts of the Apostles" be changed to the "Acts of the Holy Spirit."

After referring to the closing verses of Luke 24, "the beloved
physician" takes up the story of the ascension of the Lord Jesus
which he merely mentioned in Luke 24:51. According to Acts
1:3, Jesus ascended into Heaven forty days after His resurrection. What He did and where He was all of this time

is not told us, although He did appear to various disciples immediately after His resurrection, and then from time to time over a span of forty days. It seems that He did make daily appearances, "being seen of them forty days," and then as the time for His ascension approached He began to give His final instructions:

> And, being assembled together with them, commanded them that they should not depart from Jerusalem, but *wait* for the promise of the Father, which, saith he, ye have heard of me (Acts 1:4).

The apostles were to "stay put" in Jerusalem, and *do nothing* but *wait* for the promise of the Holy Spirit. This is a pivotal verse. Jesus said *wait* for the Holy Spirit. He knew the importance for the Church of the direction of the Holy Spirit, and commands them not to do anything *until* the Holy Spirit came to instruct them. He reminds them of the message of John:

> For John truly baptized with water; but ye shall be baptized with the Holy Ghost not many days hence (Acts 1:5).

Until then they were to *wait*. They were to make no move. They were not to act until empowered by the Holy Spirit.

The next verse (Acts 1:6) records for us another meeting. The meeting at which Jesus commanded them to wait was evidently in Jerusalem, but in verse 6 they were on the Mount of Olives. This is clear from the statement in verse 12,

> Then returned they unto Jerusalem from the mount called Olivet . . .

On the day of His ascension He led His eleven disciples out of the city of Jerusalem, past Bethany and to the Mount of Olives. Bethany was probably on the very slopes of the mountain. Luke tells us:

> And he led them out as far as to Bethany . . . (Luke 24:50).

Could it be that Jesus stopped at the home of Mary, Martha and Lazarus, to bid them a fond farewell? Why else the mention of Bethany on the way to the top of the mount? And there on the mountain the disciples asked Jesus the *last* question they were ever to ask of Him on earth. This question, and Jesus' answer, become the key to the understanding of the book of Acts. Here is the question:

> When they therefore were come together, they asked of
> him, saying, Lord, wilt thou at this time restore again the
> kingdom to Israel? (Acts 1:6).

They were on Mount Olivet, the very mountain of which
Zechariah had said:

> And his feet shall stand in that day upon the mount of
> Olives . . . (Zechariah 14:4).

The context of Zechariah 14 shows that the prophet was
speaking of the setting up of the Kingdom of Messiah upon
earth, and the establishment of the Throne of David. The
disciples understood it to mean just this, that when Messiah
came He would deliver Israel from the Gentile yoke of bondage and set up His glorious millennial Kingdom. They as yet
knew nothing about the Church. That was still a mystery, not
to be revealed until after the Holy Spirit came. They were still
looking for Jesus to set up the Kingdom, *not* to build a Church.
These disciples did not know that Israel would be set aside as
a nation for a time, and in the interval Jesus, through the Holy
Spirit, would call out the Church to be His Bride, and after
that would come again to restore the Kingdom and deliver
Israel. Since they had only the Kingdom in mind, we can understand the disciples' question:

> . . . Lord, wilt thou at this time restore again the king-
> dom to Israel? (Acts 1:6).

The question had nothing to do with the Church — it was a
question of *when Messiah's kingdom* would be set up. And note
well Jesus' answer. He did not say, "Forget about the Kingdom; the Church is going to become spiritual Israel. I am all
through with the nation of Israel. They will never be restored
as a nation, and I am not going to sit on David's Throne and
rule literally over Israel. Forget about the literal Kingdom — the
Church is now the Kingdom of God."

Jesus said nothing of the kind. If the disciples were mistaken
about the setting up of the Kingdom of Messiah upon this earth
for one thousand years, then here was the place to set them
straight, and say, "The Church is the Kingdom. God is all
through with national Israel." But Jesus did nothing of the kind.
Listen to His answer:

> . . . It is not for you to know the times or the seasons,
> which the Father hath put in his own power (Acts 1:7).

He does not deny His setting up of the Kingdom, but begins
to reveal that *before* He sets up the Kingdom, there is going to
be a lapse of time during which will be given the revelation of
the mystery — the Church. While the King delays the restoration of Israel and the setting up of the Kingdom, He is going
to carry out a hidden program, lasting over 1900 years, which
was not revealed before. This is the Church — the mystery not
made known in other ages. Before the King comes back to set
up the Kingdom, this program of gathering out the Church
must be accomplished, and so Jesus continues with a *but!*

> BUT [instead of setting up the Kingdom *now*] ye shall
> receive power, after that the Holy Ghost is come upon you:
> and ye shall be witnesses unto me both in Jerusalem, and in
> all Judea, and in Samaria, and unto the uttermost part of
> the earth (Acts 1:8).

Jesus now gives His program for the intervening age between His going away and His coming again. Instead of the
Kingdom and the restoration of one nation, Israel, He gives
a program embracing the whole world, beginning at Jerusalem
(Israel) and ending in all the world (the Gentiles). This was
Jesus' *last commission* before He left us. In this verse we have
the outline of the book of Acts, which we shall take up in our
next message. In the book of Acts the Church begins with
3,000 *Jews* — not a Gentile among them — being converted, and
the book closes with Paul turning *from* the Jews, and to the
Gentiles (Acts 28:25-28). The closing verses of Acts contain
this message, when the Jews finally rejected Paul's message.

> And when they agreed not among themselves, they de-
> parted, after that Paul had spoken one word, Well spake the
> Holy Ghost by Esaias the prophet unto our fathers,
>
> Saying, Go unto this people, and say, Hearing ye shall
> hear, and not understand; and seeing ye shall see, and not
> perceive:
>
> For the heart of this people is waxed gross, and their ears
> are dull of hearing, and their eyes have they closed; lest they
> should see with their eyes, and hear with their ears, and
> understand with their heart, and should be converted, and I
> should heal them.

> Be it known therefore unto you, that the salvation of
> God is sent unto the Gentiles, and that they will hear it
> (Acts 28:25-28).

Thus the book begins at Jerusalem with the conversion of
3,000 of the house of Israel, and the book ends in the city of
Rome with the statement, "the salvation of God is sent unto
the Gentiles, and they will hear it." This is the outline of
Acts and the program for this age.

After Jesus had given His commission to go unto all nations,
and after He had blessed them, He ascended into Heaven.
The disciples returned to Jerusalem to *wait* for further instructions, but alas! as we shall see, they couldn't wait and made the
great mistake recorded in the balance of the chapter.

May I suggest you study carefully the balance of Acts one
(Acts 1:12-26) before reading the next chapter. It will be of
immeasurable help in understanding a very controversial passage.

CHAPTER TWO

Waiting for the Promise

The book of Acts is strategically placed as the fifth book in the New Testament canon. This is not its chronological order but there can be no doubt that this is the correct dispensational order, placed as it is between the records of the gospels and the epistles. The gospels of Matthew, Mark, Luke and John record the ministry of Jesus *before* His death. The epistles record the ministry of Jesus, through the Holy Spirit, *after* His death, resurrection and ascension into Heaven. Between these two accounts of Jesus' ministry *before* Pentecost, and His ministry *after* Pentecost, we find the book of Acts. The four gospels tell us of the offer of the promised Kingdom to Israel. His message was almost exclusively to the nation of Israel. Only once did He leave the land of Palestine and that was as a Babe, fleeing from Herod the King. His message to Israel was:

> . . . Repent ye: for the kingdom of heaven is at hand (Matthew 3:2).

This was the message of John the Baptist, the forerunner of Jesus. The message was to Israel and contained the promise of the setting up of the Messianic Davidic Kingdom upon condition of national repentance. This message of John was also the message of Jesus:

> . . . Repent: for the kingdom of heaven is at hand (Matthew 4:17).

This too was the message He commissioned His disciples to preach. His command was clear and unmistakable:

> And as ye go, preach, saying, The kingdom of heaven is
> at hand (Matthew 10:17).

This was the Kingdom message and was strictly confined to
Israel, and was to be preached to Jews only. It is of the utmost
importance to remember this. After Jesus had chosen His
twelve apostles, we read in Matthew 10:5,

> These twelve Jesus sent forth, and commanded them,
> saying, Go *not* into the way of the Gentiles, and into any
> city of the Samaritans enter ye not: .
> But go rather to the lost sheep of the house of Israel (Mat-
> thew 10:5, 6).

How can anyone apply this commission to the Church or the
Gentiles, when Jesus strictly limits it to the house of Israel?
And then He tells them to heal the sick, cleanse the lepers,
raise the dead, cast out devils. These were signs related to the
Kingdom message and for Israel. To use this Scripture to support present-day healing methods and miracles is to violate the
simplest rule of Bible interpretation. It is taking the children's
meat and casting it to the dogs. Failure to see that the message
of the Kingdom in Matthew 10 was to Israel, is at the root of
all the misunderstanding concerning miracles for this age and
the disturbing confusion of tongues.

HE CAME TO HIS OWN

But this offer of the Kingdom was not accepted and so instead of sitting upon the Throne of David, He was rejected by
the nation and went to the cross instead. John says:

> He came unto his own, and his own received him not
> (John 1:11).

As a result of their rejection of their King, the nation of
Israel is to be set aside for a time (Romans 11:25), and in the
meantime God will call out a Church, the Body of Christ, to
be His Bride in the Kingdom age, when He shall come the
second time and be received by this nation and then set up
His Throne on earth. This temporary rejection of the nation
of Israel by the Lord, and the calling out of the Church in this
dispensation of Israel's setting aside was no surprise to God,
but a part of His foreknown plan. However, it was kept secret
until after the rejection of the King. The disciples of Jesus
knew very little about the calling out of the Church. All they

saw was the Kingdom, and hence the very last question asked
Him on the day of His ascension:

> . . . Lord, wilt thou at this time restore again the kingdom
> to Israel? (Acts 1:6).

Even after Pentecost it was difficult for the disciples to give up
the Kingdom idea. And right here is where the book of Acts
comes in, to bring about the transition from the Kingdom message to the message of grace. But it was a difficult lesson for
the disciples to learn. As an example of this we notice the action
of the group of disciples while waiting for the Holy Spirit to
come to guide and instruct them. After the ascension of Jesus
we read:

> Then returned they unto Jerusalem from the mount called
> Olivet, which is from Jerusalem a sabbath day's journey.
> And when they were come in, they went up into an
> upper room, where abode both Peter, and James, and John,
> and Andrew, Philip, and Thomas, Bartholomew, and Mat-
> thew, James the son of Alphaeus, and Simon Zelotes, and
> Judas the brother of James.
> These all continued with one accord in prayer and suppli-
> cation, with the women, and Mary the mother of Jesus, and
> with his brethren (Acts 1:12-14).

During the ten days between the ascension and the day of
Pentecost, the disciples were to *wait* for the Holy Spirit to give
them instructions for the carrying out of the program for the
Church. They spent their time in prayer and supplication. But
then, sometime during those ten days, impetuous, impatient
Peter had another of his wild ideas. He was still thinking of
the setting up of the Kingdom and the place of the apostles in that
Kingdom. The apostolic ministry of course was not primarily for
the Church, but had to do with the government during the reign
of Christ on earth. This had been postponed, but Peter could
not accept that idea. In this Kingdom program Jesus had
chosen *twelve* apostles, but one (Judas) had fallen by the way.
Yet in the Kingdom there must be twelve, for had not the Lord
said in Matthew 19,

> . . . when the Son of man shall sit in the throne of his
> glory, ye also (the apostles) shall sit upon twelve thrones,
> judging the twelve tribes of Israel (Matthew 19:28).

Peter had evidently remembered this. There were only eleven apostles left, and there must be twelve. While they therefore were waiting for the promise of the Spirit which Peter evidently still associated with the setting up of the Kingdom, he suggests they give the Lord a little assistance by appointing a twelfth apostle in the place of Judas. He forgot that the apostles are chosen *directly* by Christ, and are not elected by men.

PETER'S BLUNDER

Peter, unable in his impatience to wait for instructions from the Lord at Pentecost, suggests they hold an election. He recounts how Judas fell, and gives some details of his tragic end (Acts 1:15-20). And then he gives his plan, and says:

> Wherefore of these men which have companied with us all the time that the Lord Jesus went in and out among us, . . . must one be ordained to be a witness with us of his resurrection (Acts 1:21, 22).

Peter was completely out of order, for they had been commanded to *wait* for the Holy Spirit to direct them. But Peter wanted to get ready for the setting up of the Kingdom which, of course, necessitated *twelve* apostles. Since they had no revelation from God who was to be the twelfth apostle, they were forced to use carnal means for the appointment. Instead of waiting for the divine appointment of God's ordained apostle (Paul) they set up a slate of candidates and cast lots to see who would win.

> And they appointed two, Joseph called Barsabas, who was surnamed Justus, and Matthias.
>
> And they prayed, and said, Thou, Lord, which knowest the hearts of all men, shew whether of these two thou hast chosen,
>
> And they gave forth their lots; and the lot fell upon Matthias; and he was numbered with the *eleven* apostles (Acts 1:23, 24, 26).

Notice a number of things about this unauthorized procedure. First the expression, "they appointed two" (men). They did not wait for the Lord to appoint or ordain *one*, but they suggested *two* only. This limited the Lord in His choice for a twelfth apostle, to *two* men whom *they* had nominated. How did they

know it had to be one of *these* two, rather than another from the
total company of one hundred and twenty?

The next verse tells us they prayed about it, asking the Lord
to show them which of these two God had chosen. They should
have prayed about it *before* they nominated their choice. How
did they know God's chosen one was either of these two? It
is all well and good to pray for God's leading in any matter, but
to make up your mind first what you are going to do, and then
ask the Lord to put His endorsement upon *your* choice is quite
another matter. We are all too prone to make up our minds
what we want, and then try to prevail upon the Lord to yield
to our wishes. No doubt Peter and the others were sincere and
thought they were in the will of the Lord, but they had been
told to *wait* and not *act* before the Holy Spirit came to lead
them. After they had prayed for the Lord to show them which
of these two was God's choice, they still did not get an answer,
and so they were compelled to resort to the dubious method of
"chance."

THEY CAST LOTS

They had to cast lots in order to determine the choice. What
method they used we are not told, and it makes no difference.
Whether they put two names in a hat, or pulled straws, or used
some other means does not matter. They were uncertain, and
resorted to this method.

> And they gave forth their lots; and the lot fell upon Mat-
> thias; and he was numbered with the eleven apostles (Acts
> 1:16).

But it was all in vain. This was not God's choice, but man's.
The twelfth apostle would be ordained *by God,* as all the others
had been, and his name would be Paul, not Matthias. We hear
no more about Matthias. He is never again mentioned after this.
It is not said that God accepted or ordained him, or that he was
numbered among the *twelve* apostles, but with irony and re-
buke, Luke records that he was numbered with the *eleven*
apostles. Notice that — he was numbered (counted) with the
eleven, but *not with the twelve.*

PAUL'S GREAT PROBLEM

The eleven, however, would not admit their mistake, and so
continued to count Matthias among the twelve and this ac-

counts for the fact that when God's chosen apostle (Paul) came on the scene, he was not accepted as an apostle, but everywhere he went he had to defend his divine ordination as one of the twelve. In nine of the fourteen epistles he wrote, he begins with a defense of his apostleship. His place as an apostle was constantly attacked and questioned and Paul was forced to assert his authority over and over again. Notice how he introduces himself in Romans,

> Paul, a servant of Jesus Christ, called to be an apostle . . . (Romans 1:1).

He does not say "appointed by the eleven" but *called.* In I Corinthians he introduces himself in much the same manner:

> Paul, called to be an apostle of Jesus Christ through the will of God . . . (I Corinthians 1:1).

Why this emphasis on his apostleship? It was to defend himself against the charge that Matthias and not Paul was the true apostle, and so Paul adds, "I am an apostle of Jesus Christ by the will of God." The inference of course is that it was not by the will of men. In II Corinthians 1:1 we have the same introduction:

> Paul, an apostle of Jesus Christ by the will of God. . . .

In the opening verse of Galatians, however, Paul leaves no doubt why he insists upon defending his apostleship. Listen to his unmistakable words:

> Paul, an apostle, (*not of men, neither by man,* but by Jesus Christ, and God the Father, who raised him from the dead;) (Galatians 1:1).

Paul's reference to the election of Matthias in Acts 1, and his resultant rejection by the eleven is unmistakable. He says, I am "an apostle, not of men, neither by man, but of Jesus Christ." Poor Paul, he had to suffer for others' mistakes.

We need but to mention the other instances of Paul's defense of his apostleship. Ephesians opens with:

> Paul, an apostle of Jesus Christ by the will of God . . . (Ephesians 1:1).

Colossians opens in the same manner (Colossians 1:1). His first letter to Timothy opens with:

> Paul, an apostle of Jesus Christ by the commandment of
> God our Saviour, and Lord Jesus Christ. . . .

The second epistle to Timothy, and Titus also, open with his insistence upon his divine ordination as an apostle, rather than like Matthias, by the will of man.

Now this great mistake of Peter in engineering the appointment of Matthias was because he did not understand the difference between the Kingdom and the Church. And almost all the misunderstanding among believers today is for the same reason. Once we recognize the difference between the Kingdom program (now postponed) and the present program for the Church, we will be able to properly place what belongs to Israel, and what belongs to the Church. And let us not forget the practical lesson in all this. Peter's impatience was the cause of the mistake which caused Paul so much grief later. How often we in our impatience run ahead of the Lord, and also run "amuck." If in doubt, *wait!* Jesus said *wait* for the Holy Spirit to guide you. May we learn the lesson of patience. May we learn the lesson of *waiting*. God help us never to resort to carnal methods, or depend upon our fallible understanding in our zeal to promote the work of Christ. Remember that we may be sincere, but sincerely wrong. In the Bible we have God's directions and if we diligently seek for an answer from the Book, we shall not be led astray.

CHAPTER THREE

The Program for This Age

Our Lord's last commission is recorded in the first chapter of Acts:

> But ye shall receive power, after that the Holy Ghost is come upon you: and ye shall be witnesses unto me both in Jerusalem, and in all Judaea, and in Samaria, and unto the uttermost part of the earth (Acts 1:8).

This verse gives us our Lord's final commission to His disciples as well as the outline of the book of Acts, and describes the program for the Church which began at Pentecost, and will be completed at the Second Coming of Christ. It was in three stages:

1. Jerusalem and Judaea
2. Samaria
3. The uttermost part of the earth

The book of Acts is therefore easily divided according to this commission and program. The first seven chapters record the first division — the ministry of the apostles to the Jews "in Jerusalem and Judaea." They preached to no one but Jews. They did not go beyond Judaea and they still preached the message of the Kingdom. The second stage of this program "and in Samaria" is recorded in chapters 8 to 12, and marks a transition period. The Gospel now goes beyond Judaea into Samaria. It had been preached in Jerusalem to the Jew first, and now it is to go beyond Judaea. After Philip carries the message to Samaria, the third stage of the commission begins in chapter 13, with the sending forth of the first missionaries to the Gentiles. This last stage of sending the Gospel to the "uttermost part of the earth" occupies the rest of Acts, from chapter 13 to 28, and is still in the process of being carried out. The Gospel was to "the Jew first" (that is history); then to Samaria (that, too, is history); and we believe the last part, "to the uttermost part of the earth," is rapidly nearing fulfillment in this age of radio, literacy and the printed page. In the first two parts of the program, to the Jews and the Samaritans (who were half Jewish), Peter and the apostles do the preaching. In the fulfillment of the last phase, to the Gentiles — "the uttermost part of the earth," the Apostle Paul takes over the stage. We emphasize the importance of recognizing this threefold commission and its development in the book of Acts, so we repeat: (1) To Jerusalem and Judaea (Acts 1 to 7); (2) To Samaria (Acts 8 to 12); (3) To the uttermost part of the earth (Acts 13 to 28).

PREPARATION FOR THE TASK

We come now to the most important chapter in Acts, the second chapter. It records the outpouring of the Holy Spirit on the day of Pentecost, in preparing the disciples for their great task of carrying out this program to Jerusalem, Samaria, and all the earth. Failure to rightly interpret the events on this day of Pentecost will becloud the study of the rest of Acts. The right interpretation of all that follows in Acts depends upon the right interpretation of the meaning of the baptism *in* the Holy Spirit at Pentecost. The chapter opens:

> And when the day of Pentecost was fully come, they were all with one accord in one place.
>
> And suddenly there came a sound from heaven as of a rushing mighty wind, and it filled all the house where they were sitting.
>
> And there appeared unto them cloven tongues like as of fire, and it sat upon each of them.
>
> And they were all filled with the Holy Ghost, and began to speak with other tongues, as the Spirit gave them utterance (Acts 1:1-4).

This was not the first day of Pentecost. This day had been annually celebrated for hundreds of years by the nation of Israel, and this particular day recorded in Acts was the prophetic fulfillment of the typical Pentecosts which had foreshadowed the outpouring of the Spirit upon the disciples. Pentecost was one of the seven Jewish feasts mentioned in Leviticus 23, beginning with the Passover and ending with the Feast of Tabernacles. These were annual, prophetic, typical feasts, pointing forward to Christ's coming. The Passover was fulfilled at Calvary; the Unleavened Bread in His burial; the Firstfruits in His resurrection; and Pentecost was fulfilled in Acts 2.

The word "pentecost" means literally "fiftieth" so the literal translation of Acts 2:1 should be "and when the fiftieth day was fully come." Pentecost was the fiftieth day after the Feast of the Firstfruits (Leviticus 23:25, 16). So this Pentecost was to come according to the unchangeable Word of God, fifty days after the resurrection of Christ, who was our Passover (I Corinthians 5:7). There are a number of things to be observed here.

1. This Pentecost for the Church cannot be repeated in this dispensation, for the fiftieth day can never come again. It can no more be repeated in this dispensation than can the crucifixion or the burial or resurrection of Christ, which were in fulfillment of the Feasts of Passover, Unleavened Bread, and the Firstfruits. When the Spirit was poured out on Pentecost, the third Person of the Trinity came in abiding presence upon the infant Church. Jesus said of this in John 14:16,

> And I will pray the Father, and he shall give you another
> Comforter, that he may abide with you for ever;
> Even the Spirit of truth . . . (John 14:16, 17).

Pentecost for the Church was once for all. He did not come upon the company in the upper room, and then go away to be poured out over and over again upon individual believers or upon the Church. He came to *abide* (to remain) until the Church goes to meet Her Lord. In the Old Testament the Spirit came and went to empower individuals for their mission of priest or prophet or king. But in this dispensation He *abides*. To speak, therefore, of another Pentecost in this dispensation is to reveal a total misunderstanding of the experience of Pentecost.

2. The outpouring of the Spirit on Pentecost was not the result of anything the disciples did. The Spirit did not come in response to their prayers. He did not come because they were all with one accord in one place. He came because it was time for Him to come, and because Jesus had promised He would come. If they had not been with one accord in one place, if they had not been waiting, Pentecost, the fiftieth day after the Cross,

would have come anyway. How glad we are that the disciples were *in* the place where they *could* receive the Holy Spirit. Had they not been there, Pentecost would have come anyway, but they would have missed the blessing.

3. Notice also the accompanying manifestations of the Holy Spirit's coming. Three things are specifically mentioned. There was first a "sound from heaven as of a rushing mighty wind." Secondly, there were visible tongues as of fire which sat upon each (every one) of them. Thirdly, they began to speak in other languages. There are those who report present-day Pentecostal experiences, but where is the mighty wind, where are the visible tongues of fire? They claim the speaking in tongues, but before the speaking in tongues there was first the mighty rushing wind and the visible tongues as of fire. Why are not these manifestations present in the so-called present-day experiences of the baptism in the Holy Spirit? Why take only the speaking in tongues and not be able to claim the other accompanying signs — the wind and visible fire?

4. The languages these disciples spoke were not "unknown" tongues. They were existing languages understood by the people who had gathered for the feast. They needed no interpreter. This is clear when we read:

> And they were all amazed and marvelled, saying one to another, Behold, are not all these which speak Galileans?
> And how hear we every man in *our own tongue*, wherein we were born? (Acts 2:7, 8).

The Greek word translated "tongue" is *dialektos*, the same as our word "dialect." It is the same word translated "language" in verse 6.

We emphasize this point because so many people turn to the day of Pentecost for their argument for speaking in tongues. I heard one enthusiastic exponent of a repeated baptism in the Spirit say, "I received the gift of speaking in tongues the same as the disciples received on the day of Pentecost." This sincere but mistaken enthusiast simply did not understand the speaking in dialects by the disciples at Pentecost as completely distinguished from the *sign* of tongues as described in I Corinthians. Please notice, the languages used at Pentecost were languages which were spoken by the audience being addressed.

They all understood what was said. They were not unknown tongues and needed no interpretation.

This was entirely different from speaking in an unknown tongue as a sign for doubtful, carnal believers. This brings us to another observation about the Pentecostal experience.

5. The purpose of the speaking in various languages at Pentecost was in fulfillment of Jesus' command that the Gospel should begin in Jerusalem, and then go into all the world. It was to the Jews first. In the providence of God, Jews from every part of the world were present at the Feast. There were no Gentiles addressed, and among the 3,000 converted on that day there were none but Jews. I read in Acts 2:5,

> And there were dwelling at Jerusalem *Jews,* devout men, out of *every nation* under heaven (Acts 2:5).

Notice, Jews from every nation under Heaven, and at least sixteen countries are mentioned in verses 9 to 11:

> Parthians, and Medes, and Elamites, . . . Mesopotamia,
> . . . Judaea, and Cappadocia, in Pontus, and Asia,
> Phrygia, and Pamphylia, in Egypt, . . . Libya about Cyrene,
> . . . Rome, . . .
> Cretes and Arabians . . . (Acts 2:9-11).

These were all Jews or Jewish proselytes. Here they are gathered, and they are to spread the message of the Gospel to the whole world. And Pentecost was the setting for telling the story to every nation *through the Jews.* Hence the speaking in tongues. It was to proclaim the Gospel message by the nation destined to tell it to all the world. These Jews from all these nations went back to their homes all over the world knowing the message of the crucified, resurrected Christ, having heard it declared in their own language and dialect. How they failed, we shall see later.

This was the purpose of the tongues on Pentecost — to proclaim in every language the gospel message. It has nothing in common with the *sign* of tongues mentioned later in the book of I Corinthians. We repeat, therefore, that this speaking at Pentecost in the various languages was for this one occasion only, to make known the glorious Gospel to all nations, and although no Gentiles were present, the languages of the Gentile nations were heard and that from Jewish lips, indicating how in the future the whole world would again hear the Gospel through God's redeemed nation of Israel (Revelation 7).

After this day of Pentecost, this particular miracle of speaking in the well-known languages of the world was never repeated. We look in vain through the rest of Acts or the epistles for a repetition of this experience. We do find the gift of speaking in *unknown* tongues in two instances in Acts (Acts 10:46 and Acts 19:6), and it is recorded as present in only *one church* among all the churches mentioned in the book of Acts and the epistles.

SOME CONCLUSIONS

Before closing this chapter we want to make clear that in the Early Church there was the gift of speaking in unknown tongues. This we discuss later, but our purpose now is to show how this sign-gift of tongues in the Corinthian church was not a Pentecostal experience. The Pentecostal speaking in other well-known languages, understood by all, was never repeated any more than the mighty tempest or the tongues as of fire were repeated. If the miracle of addressing peoples from every nation in their own language (as it was present at Pentecost) is for us today, it would be a mighty boon in missionary work. Then it would be unnecessary for our missionaries to spend years in language study to prepare themselves for their mission. But there is no record of any missionary since Pentecost who miraculously, instantaneously could speak in the language of the people to whom they went to minister. If there is any practical value in the modern-day claim of the gift of tongues, the most useful place to exercise it would be on the foreign field. Yet the very ones who claim the gift are not able to go to the mission field without themselves spending years in learning the language of the people. More on this later, but now a practical closing word. Let us who dwell among people who understand our language, use every possible opportunity to tell the Gospel to those around us who can understand us. Until we have witnessed to all we can reach in our own language, there is no use for another, and with Paul we should say,

> Yet in the church I had rather speak five words with my understanding, that by my voice I might teach others also, than ten thousand words in an unknown tongue (I Corinthians 14:19).

CHAPTER FOUR

Speaking in Tongues

On the day of Pentecost as recorded in Acts 2, the disciples were *baptized* in the Holy Spirit. This baptism was accompanied by the sound of a mighty rushing wind and the appearance of tongues like as of fire which came and sat upon each one of them. The result of their being filled with the Spirit was the miracle of being able to address the multitude in the language and dialect of the country from which they had come. The speaking in these languages was not the evidence of the coming or baptism in the Spirit — it was the result. The evidence of the pouring out of the Spirit was wind and *fire*, and not tongues. Why do we not have the audible wind and visible tongues as of fire in the modern-day tongues movement? The one baptism in the Spirit was accompanied by these manifestations. In our former message on Pentecost we pointed out that the speaking in tongues or languages on this occasion was something quite different from the gift of speaking in unknown tongues needing an interpreter. There are only three instances of speaking in tongues in the entire book of Acts (chapters 2, 10, 19). These we shall discuss when we come to these chapters. We read not one word about this gift of tongues in connection with the other places visited by the apostles, not a word about it in Philip's ministry in Samaria, nor anywhere in the journeyings of Paul with the exception of Acts 19.

There seems to have been only one church in which the speaking in an *unknown* tongue was present. It is mentioned only in I Corinthians but not one word about it in the rest of the epistles. And note well the fact that Paul wrote to the Corinthian believers not in order to *encourage* the use of tongues, but to correct the *abuse* of this gift. It is a startling fact that the great emphasis placed on this much-abused and misunderstood gift was in the weakest and most worldly and carnal church, the church at Corinth. They were divided and split, sectarian and proud. Their spiritual knowledge was the lowest of all the churches. Most of Paul's letter was occupied with correcting abuses and evil habits and errors in walk of these childish believers. Few great doctrines are developed in Corinthians, for Paul was too busy correcting the confusion and disorder in the church.

Why Tongues In Corinth?

We would therefore ask the question: Why the emphasis on the gift of tongues in this worldly carnal group of believers? That they were given a special gift of speaking in unknown tongues is undeniable, but if the gift of tongues is an evidence of a deeper spiritual life and experience, then why in the world did God bestow this gift upon the most unspiritual church of all? If it is an evidence of spirituality, maturity and sanctification, He should have given it to the church at Ephesus or Colosse or Philippi. But there is no evidence that the believers in these churches generally made use of the gift of tongues. Why then was it so prevalent in the church of Corinth? The answer lies in their immaturity, unbelief, carnality and ignorance of the Word. Remember, these Christians did not have the New Testament Scriptures and their knowledge of truth was fragmentary. To give them additional evidence for their weak faith the Lord gave these signs. The whole answer is summed up by Paul when he says:

> Wherefore tongues are for a sign, *not to them that believe,* but to them that believe *not* . . . (I Corinthians 14:22).

To those who believed the Word of God implicitly and asked for no additional evidence than "Thus saith the Lord," no additional evidence was needed. But to the weak believers (or as Paul puts it, to them that believe not) God stoops to help them, accommodates Himself to their immature, weak faith and gives them extra evidence till they should be willing to believe His Word without signs or miracles. Remember, Paul is writing to believers — weak and stumbling believers — but *believers.* The signs, including tongues, were given to these infants in the faith as a crutch to temporarily help their faith, but as they grow in grace these crutches were not needed any more.

This gift of tongues then was especially for immature believers and was temporary. Listen to Paul as he admonishes these carnal, sign-seeking Corinthians to grow up. He says:

Brethren, be not children . . . (I Corinthians 14:20).

If people would only read the thirteenth chapter of I Corinthians before the fourteenth, they would get straightened out. This well-known chapter (I Corinthians 13) starts out:

Though I speak with the tongues of men and of angels, and have not [love], I am become as sounding brass, or a tinkling cymbal [just a big noise maker] (I Corinthians 13:1).

This chapter is called the "love" chapter, but it is really Paul's answer to the problem of signs and tongues in the Corinthian church. He is trying to show the folly of emphasizing these temporary signs and gifts above the greater gift of love. He asserts that signs, including tongues, are only for a time, during the infancy of the Church, until the full revelation of God's Word in the canon of the New Testament would be completed. And then when we have the full revelation of the Word of God, we are to cease looking for additional signs and evidences. To continue to do so is an evidence of immaturity and carnality. God today expects us to *believe His Word*, and not ask for any additional evidence. Listen to Paul in I Corinthians 13:8.

. . . whether there be prophecies [the gift of prophesying, a temporary gift before the New Testament was available], they shall fail [come to an end]; whether there be tongues, they shall cease; whether there be knowledge [special revelation], it shall vanish away.

Paul mentions three sign-gifts: prophecy, tongues, special revelation of wisdom; and says these will end when the revelation of God is complete. Notice how Paul puts it:

But when that which is perfect [complete] is come, then that which is in part shall be done away (I Corinthians 13:10).

The word "perfect" means "complete." When the revelation of the twenty-seven books of the New Testament is complete, there will be no more need of these special evidences, but we

are expected to believe God's Word just because He *says it.*
These signs and miracles were then for the days of the *infancy
of the Church,* and especially for spiritual infants, weaklings in
the faith, who needed some additional evidence instead of believing God — plus nothing. This is Paul's meaning: "Now
tongues are for a sign not to them who believe, but to them
who believe not (without some additional proof)."

God wants us to grow up to maturity by simply trusting His
Word without additional physical or emotional sensations or
experiences. These may and do often follow when we fully
trust Him implicitly. There may be a great feeling of joy, an
emotional ecstasy, as a result of basing our faith in the promises
of God, but to ask for these things before we will believe is evidence of spiritual immaturity. This is what Paul refers to in
verse 11,

> When I was a child, I spake as a child, I understood as
> a child, I thought as a child: but when I became a man, I
> put away childish things (I Corinthians 13:11).

Grow up, says Paul, and become a man of faith. No wonder the chapter ends with:

> And now abideth faith, hope, *love,* these three; but the
> greatest of these is *love* (I Corinthians 13:13).

These are the things which abide, while prophesying has
been ended, tongues have ceased, and revelation is complete.
These signs were not to abide but were for the period when
God's revelation of Scripture was not yet complete.

TEST IT BY THE WORD

Let me add a final word to this discussion, which I trust you
will receive in the same spirit in which I have tried to bring
it. My sincere motive and desire is to help you in understanding the Bible better. It is done in love and so while I respect
your views even though I may disagree, I trust you will respect
my views also and at least credit me with sincerity. Without
seeking to give offense to anyone, we would like to compare the
present-day tongues movement with the record in I Corinthians
14.

1. Tongues were the least important of all the gifts of the
Spirit in the Early Church before the New Testament was written. Paul says the gift of prophecy is far more important (I Co-

rinthians 14:1), but we hear little or nothing about this gift in these movements today, the emphasis is on the least of all the gifts — tongues.

2. The gift of tongues was for a sign to the nation of Israel, the Jews, to confirm the message of the Gospel spoken by the apostles, before the complete revelation of the written Word was given. In Mark 16:15 Jesus gives His commission to the apostles to preach the Gospel, and then adds:

> And these signs shall follow them that believe; In my name shall they cast out devils; they shall speak with new tongues;
> They shall take up serpents; and if they drink any deadly thing, it shall not hurt them; they shall lay hands on the sick, and they shall recover (Mark 16:17, 18).

These were apostolic signs of the authority of the spoken message, while there was still no written revelation and the New Testament had not yet been given. If these signs are for today, then what about taking up serpents and drinking poison? Why pick out the sign of tongues and healing, but ignore taking up snakes and drinking deadly poisons?

These signs were for the days of the transition, to confirm the message these apostles preached. This Gospel of Christ to the Church was brand new to the Jews. How could they confirm the authenticity of the message? They could not turn to Scripture, for the New Testament was not yet given.

So in the interval the Lord gave these signs to *confirm this new Message* in the absence of the *written Word of God*. This is perfectly clear from the closing verse of the gospel of Mark. After he had said these signs would be given, and He had gone to Heaven, we read:

> And they went forth, and preached every where, the Lord working with them, and *confirming the word with signs following* (Mark 16:20).

Notice the signs were to confirm the word, but now that the New Testament has been completed and confirmed by the Holy Spirit, we no longer are to look for signs before we believe; we are to believe it just because God says it.

3. The speaking in tongues was to be in an orderly fashion. Listen to Paul:

If any man speak in an unknown tongue, let it be by two,
or at the most by three, and that by course [i.e., one after another, and not two or more at the same time], and let one
interpret (I Corinthians 14:27).

It is a far cry from some of the meetings I have witnessed.
Paul says:

Let all things be done decently and in order (I Corinthians
14:40).

In the church at Corinth (the only church in which the gift
of tongues was present) no one was permitted to speak unless
there was an interpreter. Paul says:

But if there be no interpreter, let him keep silence in the
church . . . (I Corinthians 14:28).

4. We make one more observation. During the transition
period from Judaism to Christianity, the sign of tongues was
present, but it was limited to *men only.* Hear Paul's plain and
unmistakable words:

For God is not the author of confusion, but of peace, as
in all churches of the saints.
Let your women keep silence [he is referring to speaking in
tongues] in the churches: for it is not permitted unto them
to speak [in tongues]; but they are commanded to be under
obedience, as also saith the law.
. . . for it is a shame for women to speak in the church
(I Corinthians 14:33-35).

Please remember this instruction is given in the chapter dealing with tongues. Let the women keep *silence.* Here is an infallible test you may apply with confidence. In any meeting
or movement where a woman speaks in tongues it is contrary
to the Word of God, and is *not* of the Lord. Someone has said,
"Take the women out of the tongues movement and it will die."
Today with the full revelation of the Word of God it is a
sign of unbelief if we ask for anything more than "Thus saith
the Lord." If we believe His Word, we need nothing more.
If we ask for more (signs, visions, voices, miracles) we admit
we do not believe the simple Word of God. We close with
I John 5:9, 10,

If we receive the witness of men, the witness of God is
greater: for this is the witness of God which he hath testified
of his Son.

> He that believeth on the Son of God hath the witness in
> himself: he that believeth not God hath made him [God]
> a liar; because he believeth not the record that God gave
> of his Son (I John 5:9, 10).

We have the record of the Son of God. It is contained in the
twenty-seven books of the New Testament. If we will not believe that, but insist on additional proof (signs, miracles, emotions) we call God a liar, says John, "because we believe not
the record." Before the inspired record was completed God
gave signs and prophecies and revelations, but says Paul,

> . . . when that which is perfect [complete] is come, then
> that which is in part shall be done away (I Corinthians
> 13:10).

CHAPTER FIVE

The One Baptism of Ephesians 4

On the day of Pentecost, occurring fifty days after the resurrection of Christ and ten days after His ascension, the person of the Holy Spirit was poured out upon a company of 120 believers in an upper room in Jerusalem as they waited the baptism in the Holy Spirit. Jesus had promised this event just before He ascended into Heaven. He said:

> For John truly baptized with [IN] water; but ye shall be baptized with [IN] the Holy Ghost not many days hence (Acts 1:5).

This promise is repeated in Acts 1:8,

> But ye shall receive power, after that the Holy Ghost is come upon you: and ye shall be witnesses unto me both in Jerusalem, and in all Judea, and in Samaria, and unto the uttermost part of the earth.

Ten days after this, the promise was fulfilled. As they were assembled in one place,

> . . . suddenly there came a sound from heaven as of a rushing mighty wind, and it filled all the house where they were sitting.
>
> And there appeared unto them cloven tongues like as of fire, and it sat upon each of them.
>
> And they were all filled with the Holy Ghost, and began to speak with other tongues, as the Spirit gave them utterance (Acts 2:2-4).

This was the fulfillment of the promise of Jesus that they would be *baptized in the Holy Ghost*. It happened on Pentecost, the entire person of the Spirit came upon the infant Church to *abide*. Pentecost is past — it cannot be repeated until the Spirit has taken the Church home again in the Rapture. Unless we distinguish between the ministry of the Holy Spirit in the Old Testament before Pentecost, and the peculiar ministry of the Holy Spirit *after* Pentecost, nothing but confusion can result. In the Old Testament the Spirit came and went, but not to abide and remain. He came upon certain individuals to equip and prepare them for special service and office. Thus He came upon priests and prophets and kings to fit them for their work. After they had finished their work, the Spirit could then again be withdrawn. As an illustration we call attention to Saul, the first king of Israel. After he had been anointed by Samuel, the prophet says to Saul:

> And the Spirit of the LORD will come upon thee, and thou shalt prophesy with them, and shalt be turned into another man (I Samuel 10:6).

This was immediately fulfilled, and we read in verse 10,

> . . . and the Spirit of God came upon him, and he prophesied among them.

This enduement with the Spirit was to prepare and fit him for the task of ruling Israel. But Saul was disobedient to the Spirit's command and rebelled against God and as a result we now read in I Samuel 16:14,

> But the Spirit of the LORD departed from Saul, and an evil spirit from the LORD troubled him.

Before Pentecost the Spirit came upon individuals for the definite purpose of equipping them for a specific task, and the Spirit could depart when the recipient was disobedient, or when his work was done. As a result the Spirit left Saul when God rejected him as king. It had nothing to do with Saul's salvation. It pertained only to his office as king. God now chooses David to be king, and we read in verse 13:

> Then Samuel took the horn of oil, and anointed him [David] in the midst of his brethren: and the *Spirit of the Lord* came upon David from that day forward . . .
> But the Spirit of the LORD departed from Saul . . . (I Samuel 16:13, 14).

David also realized that he had received the Spirit for the office of king, upon condition of obedience, and so he prays in Psalm 51:11,

> . . . take not thy holy spirit from me.

Now He Comes to Abide

The coming of the Holy Spirit on Pentecost was entirely different. Now He comes to *stay* to the end of the age, dwelling *in* the Body of Christ and in the individual believers. This is what Jesus declared in His promise in John 14,

> And I will pray the Father, and he shall give you another Comforter, that he may abide with you for ever;
> Even the Spirit of truth; whom the world cannot receive, because it seeth him not, neither knoweth him: but ye know him; for he *dwelleth with you,* and *shall be in you* (John 14:16, 17).

Notice carefully the expression, "he *dwelleth with you,* and *shall be in you.*"

This was before Pentecost and the Spirit was already *with* the disciples just as He had always been in the Old Testament. When Jesus spoke these words the Spirit did not *indwell* the disciples, but was *with them,* for He is omnipresent. But then Jesus adds, *"and shall be in you."* This pointed to the time when the Spirit would come to abide.

This happened at Pentecost. Here the Spirit came to *abide* and *dwell* in the newborn Church. The Spirit of God is not given by measure (John 3:34). We cannot dissect the Spirit of God or divide Him into portions, as though only a part of the Spirit was poured out upon the 120 in the upper room, and now pours out a little more here and there upon this one and that one. *No!* The entire person of the Spirit came on Pentecost to live in this world in a *body* which is the Church of Christ. He has not gone back, and will not go back until that "body" born as an infant of 120 members is completed and He takes it to Heaven.

Only One Baptism

This outpouring of the Spirit on Pentecost is the *one baptism* of Ephesians 4:

> There is one body, and one Spirit . . .
> One Lord, one faith, one baptism,
> One God and Father of all, who is above all, and through all, and *in you all* (Ephesians 4:4-6).

As there is only *one body,* the true Church, and only one Spirit, only one Lord, so there can be only one baptism. It is history! That baptism was upon the infant Church in the upper room. Pentecost may be called the *birthday* of the Holy Spirit, just as logically as we talk about the birthday of Jesus. Of course, Jesus always was the eternal, omnipresent, pre-existent Son of God, but nineteen hundred years ago He took on a body and dwells today in that human body. This event we call the birthday of Jesus, because then He came to dwell in a body. In the same way the Holy Spirit also always was, for He is the eternal, omnipresent, pre-existent Spirit of God, but on Pentecost He entered a body, the Body of Christ, the Church, and so we may call it the *birthday* of the Holy Spirit, because on that day the body whom He indwells was born.

That infant body, consisting of only 120 believers was the complete body of Christ. Although countless millions of members were to be added to that body in the centuries which followed, that body of 120 believers on Pentecost represented the entire Church, the body of all believers in every age. Just as God saw all believers represented in the body of Christ as He hung on the cross and reckoned that what happened to that body, happened to all believers, so too on the day of Pentecost. When God looked upon the body of Jesus on the cross He saw a spiritual body consisting of all the members who would still be added in the centuries to come. What happened to the body of Jesus happened to every member. Paul says,

> . . . we are members of his (Christ's) body, of his flesh, and of his bones (Ephesians 5:30).

And in Galatians 2:20:

> I am [have been] crucified with Christ, nevertheless I live.

God saw in the crucifixion of Christ every member of that spiritual body (the Church) for which He died. So Paul could say, "I was crucified with Christ" (Galatians 2:20); "I was buried with him" (Romans 6:4); "I was raised with Christ" (Ephesians 2:5, 6); and "am ascended and seated with him" (Ephesians 2:6). In Christ the Church is complete in the eyes of God, for He saw every member of that body from eternity, "chosen in him from before the foundation of the world" (Ephesians 1:4). In the eyes of God and according to His foreknowledge the little company at Pentecost was *the* Church, the complete body of Christ. We may take the example of a newborn infant. It is small, weak and helpless, but it is a child of its parents as much the moment it is born as it will be forty years later. Its relationship to its father is complete at birth. But while complete in relationship, it is still incomplete in development. It must still add thousands upon thousands of cells before it is full grown from a baby of seven or eight pounds to a mature man of 175 pounds, more or less. The infant is complete and incomplete – complete as a person, a son, a member of the family; but incomplete in development. The whole future man is in that infant.

Whole Body Baptized

In the same way the little company of believers on Pentecost was the Church, the complete infant Church, but it still needed billions of members added experientially, although God already saw those members in the little body of believers at Pentecost. Upon this body, the Church, the person of the Holy Spirit was poured out. Every believer in the following centuries was represented there and was baptized with that body in the Holy Spirit. Every member of the Body of Christ was in God's sight baptized once for all at Pentecost. It can never be repeated for the Church. And now when a sinner repents and believes and is saved, the Holy Spirit is not poured out upon that believer, but instead he is at that moment experientially introduced into the already baptized Body of Christ, just as new cells are added to the growing infant's body. What happens to the baby happens to the man. Our baptism was accomplished nineteen hundred years ago, and we become partakers of it by experience when we accept Christ. Paul clinches the matter in one all-convincing verse in I Corinthians 12:13,

> For by [IN] one Spirit are we all [literally WERE WE ALL]
> baptized into one body, . . . and have been all made to drink
> into one Spirit.

Paul says some 25 years after Pentecost, "I was baptized in the Spirit on that day." I was there as a member of that body in the mind of God, so that Paul could say, "I was baptized together with all believers once for all," just as positively as he could say, "I was crucified with Christ." Paul did not physically die on the cross, but was represented in the body of Christ. So Paul too was not physically present at Pentecost, but was represented in the body of those believers.

We have dwelt at length on this truth of *one body, one Spirit, one Lord, one faith, one baptism,* because it is the only key to the proper understanding of the significance of Pentecost.

BAPTISM AND FILLING

The cause of so much misunderstanding of this subject among believers is a failure or an unwillingness to distinguish between *baptism in* and *filling with* the Spirit. Many sincere believers experience the filling of the Holy Spirit in response to obedience, yielding and confession, and mistake that experience and joy of being filled for the *one baptism.* Filling with the Spirit may be repeated as often as we yield to the Spirit's leading, but Paul says "there is *one* baptism"; viz., the pouring out of the Spirit on Pentecost, of which our water baptism is only a symbol. When we submit to baptism we thereby testify that we have already been baptized in the Spirit, and by faith are members of the Body of Christ. Before we close we mention one more thing about this baptism at Pentecost.

WHO IS THE BAPTIZER?

The disciples at Pentecost were not baptized *by* the Holy Spirit. There is no baptism *by* the Spirit, but rather a baptism *in* the Spirit. Jesus is the Baptizer. He is the One who poured out the Spirit and did the baptizing. If you doubt this, then read the following words by John the Baptist:

> I indeed baptize you with [IN] water unto repentance: but he that cometh after me is mightier than I, whose shoes I am not worthy to bear: *he shall baptize you* with the Holy Ghost, and with fire (Matthew 3:11).

Who is the baptizer? *Jesus!* This is repeated by Luke.

> . . . he [Jesus] shall baptize you with the Holy Ghost and with fire (Luke 3:16).

This is again repeated by John in John 1:33. These promises were all carried out on the day of Pentecost. To be saved, one need not tarry and wait and plead for the Holy Spirit to be poured out, but all one must do is repent of his sins, believe the Gospel, confess Jesus as Lord and trust His promise. By the experience of salvation one is thus introduced into the body of Christ as one of the members of that body, already baptized in the Spirit nineteen hundred years ago, and reckoned by God as a chosen one from eternity (Ephesians 1:4). If you have not been baptized in the Spirit you are *lost*. There is no baptism in the Spirit *after* you are saved, for if you are saved you have the Spirit dwelling in you. You either have the Spirit or you do not have Him. Paul leaves no doubt about this, and says:

> . . . Now if any man have not the Spirit of Christ, he is none of his (Romans 8:9).

There is one Body. Do you belong to it?
There is one Spirit. Is He yours?
There is one Lord. Have you owned Him?
There is one Faith. Have you received it?
There is one Baptism. Have you experienced it?
There is one God and Father. Do you know Him?

> There is one body, and one Spirit, even as ye are called in one hope of your calling;
> One Lord, one faith, one baptism,
> One God and Father of all, who is above all, and through all, and in you all (Ephesians 4:4-6).

CHAPTER SIX

Peter's First Sermon

On the day of Pentecost, 120 disciples were baptized *in* the Holy Spirit, by the Lord Jesus Christ. Immediately they were enabled to speak the Gospel to the multitude who had assembled from practically every country under Heaven. They heard the message in their own tongue or dialect, so that as these visitors returned to their native country they could have evangelized the whole world in that first century. When these disciples stood up and preached in these various languages it created quite a stir. We read:

> And they were all mazed, and were in doubt, saying one to another, What meaneth this?
> Others mocking said, These men are full of new wine (Acts 2:12, 13).

Then Peter answers them and delivers his first sermon at Pentecost. Peter's answer to the scoffers begins with a reference to the prophecy of the outpouring of the Holy Spirit:

> But Peter, standing up with the eleven, lifted up his voice, and said unto them, Ye men of Judaea, and all ye that dwell at Jerusalem, be this known unto you, and hearken to my words:
> For these are not drunken, as ye suppose, seeing it is but the third hour of the day.
> But this is that which was spoken by the prophet Joel;
> And it shall come to pass in the last days, saith God, I will pour out of my Spirit upon all flesh: and your sons and daughters shall prophesy, and your young men shall see visions, and your old men shall dream dreams:
> And on my servants and on my handmaidens I will pour out in those days of my Spirit; and they shall prophesy:

And I will shew wonders in heaven above, and signs in
the earth beneath; blood, and fire, and vapour of smoke:

The sun shall be turned into darkness, and the moon into
blood, before that great and notable day of the Lord come:

And it shall come to pass, that whosoever shall call on the
name of the Lord shall be saved (Acts 2:14-21).

Peter quotes to them from the prophecy of Joel 2:28 to 32.
Notice a number of things concerning this prophecy of the outpouring of the Spirit:

1. It will be in the last days.

2. It will be after the defeat of the armies of Russia (Joel 2:
19, 20).

3. The Spirit will be poured upon all flesh (Joel 2:28).

4. It will be accompanied by fire, blood and smoke.

5. The sun will be blackened, and the moon shall be turned
to blood.

Now none of these things happened at Pentecost. Yet Peter
quotes this prophecy to explain what happened at Pentecost.
But he does not say this is the *fulfillment* of the prophecy of
Joel. He did not use the word "fulfilled" at all. He could not
say this prophecy was fulfilled, for the complete fulfillment
of Joel's prophecy will come *after* the Church is raptured. And
so Peter says "this is *that*" which was spoken by Joel. It was
only part of the complete prophecy. Pentecost was only the
earnest, the first step, of what will take place when Joel's prophecy is fulfilled, just before the Second Coming of the King to
set up His Kingdom on earth. On the day of Pentecost the
Spirit was not poured out upon *all* flesh, but only on the Church.
On that day there were not the signs of blood and fire and
smoke. On that day the sun was not darkened and the moon
did not turn to blood. All that still. awaits fulfillment. These
signs have never yet happened, either at Pentecost or since,
even though some speak of repeating Pentecost. The fulfillment
of Joel's prophecy *began* at Pentecost, was interrupted until
after the Church is gone and Israel owns her Messiah, and then
at the Second Coming of the Spirit all will be fulfilled.

Now the Gospel

After Peter has explained the strange happenings to the
assembled crowd, he brings to them the message of the Gospel.
We suggest you read all of Peter's sermon on this day as re-

corded in Acts 2:14 to 36. We would point out three important things about Peter's sermon:

1. It was addressed to *Jews* only. It was the gospel message of the Kingdom exclusively for the nation of Israel. It was addressed to none other than to Israelites. He introduces his sermon with:

> . . . Ye men of Judaea, and all ye that dwell in Jerusalem (Acts 2:14).

> Ye men of Israel, hear these words . . . (Acts 2:22).

> Men and brethren [Israelites], let me freely speak unto you of the patriarch David . . . Acts 2:29).

> Therefore let all the house of Israel know assuredly, that God hath made that same Jesus, whom ye [Israel] have crucified, both Lord and Christ (Acts 2:36).

The entire message was addressed to Israel, and, as we shall see, was the offer of the Kingdom which they had once refused. They are to receive a second offer, and when this too is refused, the Gospel goes out into all the Gentile world. But the order of Christ's commission was *first* in Jerusalem and Judaea, to the nation of Israel; then to Samaria; and finally, to the uttermost part of the earth. Peter's first sermon was preached in Jerusalem and addressed to "Ye men of Israel." It was to Jews only.

2. Notice next the message. Peter was led to bring to Israel the message of the rejected Christ. He quotes freely from the Old Testament with which the hearers were familiar and then goes on to proclaim the Gospel — the message of a crucified, buried, risen Christ. The heart of Peter's message is in the words found in verses 22 to 24:

> Ye men of Israel [notice to whom he addresses his words], hear these words; Jesus of Nazareth, a man approved of God among you by miracles and wonders and signs, which God did by him in the midst of you, as ye yourselves also know:

> Him, being delivered by the determinate counsel and knowledge of God, ye have taken, and by wicked hands have crucified and slain:

> Whom God raised up, having loosed the pains of death: because it was not possible that he should be holden of it (Acts 2:22-24).

This was the message of the Gospel to the nation of Israel, the message of a crucified but risen Messiah. Then he quotes

from David to show that this truly was the Messiah King whom
they had rejected and slain.

3. We come now to the result. Under the power of the message great conviction fell upon the multitude.

> Now when they heard this, they were pricked in their
> heart, and said unto Peter and to the rest of the apostles,
> Men and brethren, what shall we do?
>
> Then Peter said unto them, Repent, and be baptized every
> one of you in the name of Jesus Christ for the remission of
> sins, and ye shall receive the gift of the Holy Ghost (Acts
> 2:37, 38).

Notice Peter's answer to their question, "What shall we do?"
He says, "Repent, and be baptized." These two things were the
requisites for the remission of sins and receiving the Holy
Ghost. To use this passage for the Church today leads to utter
confusion. To apply these words to us today results in the common error of making water baptism a requirement for salvation.
That would mean baptismal regeneration, which is a denial of
the Gospel of salvation by grace. This was not the message of
Paul to the Philippian jailer when he cried out, "Sirs, what must
I do to be saved?" Paul did not say, "Repent, and be baptized,"
but instead he said, "Believe on the Lord Jesus Christ, and thou
shalt be saved" (Acts 16:31). The Philippian jailor was not
a Jew, but a Gentile. Notice the use of the pronoun in Acts
2 and in Acts 16. At Pentecost the plural pronoun is used,
"What shall *we* do?" What must *we* as a *nation* do? But in the
case of the Philippian jailor, the singular first person pronoun
is used, "What must I do to be saved?"

The reason for Peter's answer, "Repent, and be baptized,"
was because he was speaking to the very people who had openly
rejected Jesus. They must therefore also openly acknowledge and
own Him as their Messiah. They must repent and manifest this
by being baptized in the name of Jesus Christ. Why not in the
name of the Father, Son and Holy Ghost? This was not necessary! They already believed in the Father and in the Holy Ghost,
but they must now assert their faith in Jesus Christ whom they
had rejected. Baptism was for these Jews a condition to prove
they had repented of their rejection of Jesus.

4. One more observation about Peter's sermon. He mentions
a promise, and says,

> For the promise is unto you, and to your children, and to
> all that are afar off . . . (Acts 2:39).

The offer must first be made to the nation of Israel, and after
that the message would go into Samaria and unto the uttermost
part of the earth. If the nation of Israel had received this second
offer of the Kingdom, their Messiah would have returned; but
God knew this offer would also be rejected, and so planned
His program for the Church after the Gospel had been given
to the Jew first, and rejected by them.

THE EARLY CHURCH

Three thousand souls were added to the Church of 120 members baptized that day in the Holy Spirit. It does *not* say these
three thousand were baptized into the body of Christ, but they
were added to the already baptized body of believers. And
then follows a brief picture of an Early Church meeting:

> And they continued stedfastly in the apostles' doctrine
> and fellowship, and in breaking of bread, and in prayers.
> And fear came upon every soul: and many wonders and
> signs were done by the apostles (Acts 2:42, 43).

The church meeting of the first century was the essence of
simplicity. Four things are mentioned in particular. It was
characterized by:

1. Bible study — apostles' doctrine
2. Fellowship — testimony
3. Breaking of bread — remembering the Lord
4. Prayers

Being led by the Holy Spirit, there was a complete absence of
complexity. There was a bare minimum of organization, of
boards, committees, programs or gadgets. There was no specified
ritual, no program of entertainment, no pictures or elaborate
preliminaries. Just a company of born again believers led by
the Holy Spirit to listen to the Word, give their testimony, remember the Lord and pray; and then go out everywhere witnessing for their Lord and Christ. It surely is a far cry from the simplicity of that gathering to the highly organized pageantry and
promotional machinery of the modern church today. No wonder
we are so powerless!

BIBLE COMMUNISM

The second chapter of Acts closes with a picture of *Bible communism*, which is as different from what we call communism today as Heaven is from hell.

> And all that believed were together, and had all things common;
> And sold their possessions and goods, and parted them to all men, as every man had need (Acts 2:44, 45).

This passage has been greatly abused and even distorted by modern-day communists. These disciples pooled all their possessions and distributed them as every man had need. Is this order for today? Are we as Christians to practice this order? Few there are who would answer "yes." Those who have nothing to share might say "yes." How then can we explain this practice in the Early Church? It is easily explained, if you remember:

1. This is the Kingdom ideal. The apostles were still offering the Kingdom to Israel, and in the Millennium when Christ shall be King, this will be the voluntary rule. There will be no poverty; everyone will have enough, by equal distribution of God's physical blessings when every man shall sit under his own vine and his own fig tree.

2. These early Christians were a despised company. They were persecuted and ignored, slighted and disregarded by the world. They were waiting for Messiah to return and set up the Kingdom, and so they formed this *community* program.

3. This was not mandatory, but entirely on a voluntary basis. No one was forced to share all his possessions with others. It was not obligatory but was only for those who desired to do so. This is made plain later in chapter 5, in the case of Ananias and Sapphira who sold their possessions and brought them to the apostles. However, they lied about it. They pretended to have brought *all* of their possessions, while they secretly held back part of it.

Peter's answer declares that this practice was not required but was entirely up to the individual. He says, why did you

> . . . keep back part of the price of the land?
> Whiles it remained [unsold], was it not thine own? and after it was sold, was it not in thine own power [to do as you pleased]? (Acts 5:3, 4).

This was a practice while the hope of the Kingdom was burning brightly and it will work in the Kingdom Age when every knee shall bow to Christ. But to teach that this practice is for today is quite foolish. It was all perfectly proper in *Jerusalem.* If you are one of those who believe that this practice of selling all and laying it at the apostles' feet is for us today, then why don't you start off by doing it? There is no law against it. It is entirely voluntary and no one will object. We must be very careful to rightly divide the Word of God. While the message was still to Jerusalem all this was perfectly proper. We may, however, make a practical application.

The Christian today should recognize that all that he has is the gift of God and he is responsible for the way he uses it. We are to invest what we have in things spiritual as well as necessary physical needs. But this holds true not only in the matter of our material possessions but our time and talents and testimony as well. The amount you are willing to give to the Lord depends upon your love for Christ, your gratitude to God, and the joy the true believer experiences in laying everything at His feet.

. . . Let every man be fully persuaded in his own mind (Romans 14:5).

CHAPTER SEVEN

Israel's Second Chance

The third chapter of Acts records the second sermon preached by the Apostle Peter. It opens with a miracle by Peter, in the healing of a lame man at the gate of the Temple. The lame man healed of his paralysis, leaped upon his feet and ran into the Temple praising God. This soon brought together a great crowd and Peter saw the opportunity of preaching to them.

> And when Peter saw it, he answered unto the people, *Ye men of Israel,* why marvel ye at this? (Acts 3:12).

Notice how Peter addresses them, "Ye men of Israel," and later he says:

> The God of *Abraham,* and of *Isaac,* and of *Jacob,* the God of *our* fathers, hath glorified his *Son* Jesus; whom ye delivered up, and denied him in the presence of Pilate, . . .
> And killed the Prince of life, whom God hath raised from the dead; whereof we are witnesses.
> And his name through faith in his name hath made this man strong (Acts 3:13, 15, 16).

Again notice the outstanding elements in this record of Peter's second sermon: 1. The scene is the Temple, even though the Temple was already abandoned by God. But since the Jews still frequented the Temple, and Peter's message was still directed to the nation of Israel, the proper place was the Temple.

2. The message was still to the Jews, the nation of Israel. The invitation was still to Jerusalem and Judaea. This is perfectly clear in the record. He addresses them:

> Ye men of Israel, why marvel ye at this? (Acts 3:12).

In verse 13 he addresses them as follows:

> The God of Abraham, and of Isaac, and of Jacob, the God of our fathers.

Later he tells them:

> Ye are the children of the prophets, and of the covenant which God made with our fathers, saying unto Abraham, And in thy seed shall all the kindreds of the earth be blessed.
> Unto you [Jews] *first* God, having raised up his Son Jesus, sent him to bless you . . . (Acts 3:25, 26).

The message was addressed again to the nation of Israel for it was to be *to the Jews first*, and this was fulfilled in the book of Acts.

THE SECOND INVITATION

This message had been offered once and according to God's foreknown plan was rejected by the nation. Peter says:

> And now, brethren, I wot not that through ignorance ye did it, as did also your rulers.
> But those things, which God before had shewed by the mouth of all his prophets, that Christ should suffer, he hath so fulfilled (Acts 3:17, 18).

And then Peter repeats the invitation to the nation of Israel. It is the second invitation after Pentecost.

> Repent ye therefore, and be converted, that your sins may be blotted out, when the times of refreshing shall come from the presence of the Lord;
> And he shall send Jesus Christ, which before was preached unto you:
> Whom the heaven must receive until the times of restitution of all things, which God hath spoken by the mouth of all his holy prophets since the world began (Acts 3:19-21).

This was Peter's message to Israel. It was the promise of the Kingdom, upon condition of their repentance and acknowledgment of Jesus as their Messiah. If they had accepted this invitation, Jesus their Messiah would have immediately returned from Heaven to set up the Davidic Kingdom. It would have ushered in the promised "time of refreshing" (verse 19). Peter says if you will repent, then God "shall send Jesus Christ, which before was preached unto you" (Acts 3:20). But God foreknew this invitation too would be rejected and so Peter adds:

Whom [Jesus] the heaven must receive *until* the times
of restitution of all things, which God hath spoken . . .
(Acts 3:21).

Since the nation would not receive this repeated offer, Jesus
will remain in Heaven *until* (notice the word *until*) the times
of restitution of all things. This refers to the time when Israel
will be converted and their Messiah will come and set up His
Kingdom. This is what Paul later states in Romans 11,

. . . that blindness in part is happened to Israel, *until* the
fulness of the Gentiles be come in.
And so [then] all Israel shall be saved: as it is written,
There shall come out of Sion the Deliverer, and shall turn
away ungodliness from Jacob (Romans 11:25, 26).

We ask the question, What would have happened if Israel
had repented at Peter's message? Undoubtedly all would have
come to pass in rapid succession and Christ would have returned
for the "times of refreshing, and the restitution of all things."
But this was not in the purpose of God. He knew Israel would
reject this offer also, for so it had been foretold. The Kingdom
is to be postponed, and the mystery age of the Church would fill
the gap between Israel's rejection at Christ's first coming and
their acceptance of Him at the Second Coming. God's purpose for the Church, the body of Christ, must be carried out
while Israel is in rejection. Then after the Church Age is complete, Israel *will* be converted and the glorious Kingdom Age be
ushered in.

TAUGHT IN PARABLE

This program was not only foretold by the prophets, but also
taught in parable by Jesus. In Matthew 22 Jesus speaks to the
leaders of Israel after they had tried to kill Him (Matthew
21:46). Then Jesus says:

The kingdom of heaven is like unto a certain king, which
made a marriage for his son,
And sent forth his servants to call them that were bidden to
the wedding: and they would not come.
Again, he sent forth other servants, saying, Tell them which
are bidden, Behold, I have prepared my dinner: my oxen
and my fatlings are killed, and all things are ready: come
unto the marriage.
But they made light of it, and went their ways . . .
(Matthew 22:2-5).

Notice that here are two separate invitations to the king's dinner for his son. The king is the Father; the king's son is Jesus Christ; the guests who were bidden *first* are the nation of Israel. The first invitation was by the king's servants *before* the feast was ready. The servants were the prophets and the apostles sent to the nation of Israel to honor the *son* by coming to the feast. But they refused the invitation. The second is again to the same company who were bidden first. This invitation was *after* the dinner was ready. The sacrificial animals had been slain, the feast was waiting. This is the invitation *after* the Cross and *after* Pentecost. The invitation is by Peter and the other disciples and is recorded in these two chapters of Acts. Once more the Kingdom is offered and the Kingdom is once again promised when he "shall send Jesus Christ, which *before* was preached unto you." But this second offer was also rejected. They abused the servants who brought the message as recorded in the next chapter of Acts (Acts 4). Jesus predicted this in the parable:

> And the remnant took his servants, and entreated them spitefully, and slew them (Matthew 22:6).

The servants who with Peter preached to the nation after Pentecost were persecuted, culminating in the stoning of Stephen in Acts, chapter 7. The invitation was to Israel *first*, beginning at Jerusalem. But when this final invitation was rejected, the nation comes under judgment and Jesus predicts it in these prophetic words:

> But when the king heard thereof, he was wroth: and he sent forth his armies, and destroyed those murderers, and burned up their city (Matthew 22:7).

This was literally fulfilled when the Roman legions marched upon Jerusalem under Titus in the year A.D. 70 and deported the nation and burned the city of Jerusalem with fire. The bidden ones, the chosen guests, are punished and now the invitation goes to the hitherto *unbidden* guests. After the rejection by the favored guests we read:

> Then saith he to his servants, The wedding is ready, but they which were bidden were not worthy.
> Go ye therefore into the highways, and as many as ye shall find, bid to the marriage (Matthew 22:8, 9).

WHOSOEVER WILL MAY COME

The invitation is now extended to "whosoever will." The message of the Gospel, rejected by the nation, now is to go into all the world. Salvation has burst beyond national walls and the commission of our Lord was literally carried out. Jesus had said,

... in Jerusalem, and in all Judaea, and in Samaria, and unto the uttermost part of the earth (Acts 1:8).

The first part of this commission was fulfilled in the first seven chapters of Acts, and was concluded when Stephen was stoned. Then followed the second step, "and in Samaria," when Philip went into Samaria and preached the Gospel there (Acts 8). And now we are ready for the third stage, "unto the uttermost part of the earth," — "into the highways and byways," to bid whosoever will to come. This third stage is introduced by the conversion of Paul in Acts 9. After Peter opens the door to the Gentiles in chapter 10, he steps out of the picture, and Paul, the apostle to the Gentiles, takes the spotlight. The ministry of the apostles "to Israel *first*" comes to a close. With the beginning of the first missionary journey in Acts 13 we enter upon the third and final step in witnessing *first* in Jerusalem, next in Samaria, and then to the uttermost part of the earth. This third stage is still in progress and will end at the Rapture of the Church, and then God will once more begin to deal with the nation of Israel. The chapter ends with Peter's declaration of this order of events:

Unto you [Israel] *first* God, having raised up his Son Jesus, sent him to bless you, in turning away every one of you from his iniquities (Acts 3:26).

The next chapter opens with the account of how the servants of the King were treated by those to whom the invitation was *first* given. It records the first great persecution:

And as they spake unto the people, the priests, and the captain of the temple, and the Sadducees, came upon them,
And they laid hands on them, and put them in hold unto the next day: for it was now eventide (Acts 4:1, 3).

The rejection of Peter's message now becomes official. The rulers of the nation now take counsel against them.

And it came to pass on the morrow, that their rulers, and elders, and scribes,

> And Annas the high priest, and Caiaphas, and John, and
> Alexander, and as many as were of the kindred of the high
> priest, were gathered together at Jerusalem.
> And when they had set them in the midst, they asked, By
> what power, or by what name, have ye done this? [referring
> to the healing of the lame man on the previous day] (Acts
> 4:5-7).

Once more Peter, for the third time, bears testimony for his
Lord and this time before the official meeting of the Sanhedrin,
the ruling party of Israel. Again the message is addressed to
Israel, and he says:

> . . . Ye rulers of the people, and elders of Israel,
> Be it known unto you all, and to all the people of Israel
> . . . (Acts 4:8, 10).

Again the message is the same — the death and the resurrection of Jesus. Again he accuses them of rejecting their Messiah,
and quotes from Psalm 118:22.

> This is the stone which was set at nought of *you* builders,
> which is become the head of the corner (Acts 4:11).

The stone was their Messiah and King upon acceptance of
whom the Kingdom was to be set up, but now is to become the
head of the corner of the Church. Jesus the stone rejected by
the nation is now to become the *cornerstone* of the Church, the
body of Christ. While Peter declares the rejection of the nation, he now also proclaims personal salvation. As a nation Israel is set aside, while any individual who receives Jesus will
be saved. It is now to be *individual*, personal salvation, and
so Peter concludes with the invitation to any individual to receive Christ. Hear Peter's invitation:

> Neither is there salvation in any other: for there is none
> other name under heaven given among men, whereby we must
> be saved (Acts 4:12).

The Gospel message to the whole world is introduced in this
verse. From now on the invitation will be to "whosoever will,"
whether he be Jew or Gentile. The Apostle Paul confirms this
in Acts 13:45, 46. He is addressing the people of Israel in Antioch,
but they refused to hear and Luke records:

> But when the Jews saw the multitudes, they were filled
> with envy, and spake against those things which were spoken

by Paul, contradicting and blaspheming.

Then Paul and Barnabas waxed bold, and said [now notice] It was necessary that the word of God should *first* have been spoken to you: but seeing ye put it from you, and judge yourselves unworthy of everlasting life, *lo, we turn to the Gentiles.*

For so hath the Lord commanded us, saying, I have set thee to be a light of the Gentiles, that thou shouldest be for salvation unto the ends of the earth.

And when the Gentiles heard this, they were glad, and glorified the word of the Lord: and as many as were ordained to eternal life believed.

And the word of the Lord was published throughout all the region (Acts 13:45-49).

CHAPTER EIGHT
Bible Communism

The first seven chapters of the book of Acts record for us the ministry of the Apostle Peter and the other apostles to the nation of Israel exclusively. The scene is limited to the city of Jerusalem, the message is the Gospel of a crucified, risen Christ. If Israel had accepted the message through their rulers, the glorious Kingdom age of peace would have been ushered in by the return of Israel's Messiah (Acts 3:19-21). Instead of repenting of their sin, they haled the apostles before the Sanhedrin, the official ruling body of the nation. The apostles spent a night in jail and the next day answered the charges against them by once more preaching the rejected Messiah in spite of the fact they were commanded not to speak at all, nor teach in the name of Jesus (Acts 4:13-22). But instead of silencing them it only increased their boldness and they went back to their own company praising God; and in answer to prayer they were again filled with the Holy Ghost for still greater service (Acts 4:31).

THE HAPPY ASSEMBLY

This fourth chapter of Acts closes with a delightful picture of the Early Church united together in the face of increased persecution. This picture is one of devotion, love, unity and joy.

> And the multitude of them that believed were of one heart and of one soul: neither said any of them that ought of the things which he possessed was his own; but they had all things common.
>
> Neither was there any among them that lacked: for as many as were possessors of lands or houses sold them, and brought the prices of the things that were sold,
>
> And laid them down at the apostles' feet: and distribu-

tion was made unto every man according as he had need.
And Joses, who by the apostles was surnamed Barnabas, . . .
Having land, sold it, and brought the money, and laid it
at the apostles' feet (Acts 4:32, 34-37).

Is This for Us Today?

Again we ask the question, "Is this practice applicable for
us today?" Those who take everything in the book of Acts as
being a pattern for the Church in this age would have difficulty
here. I would ask those who claim that the signs and miracles
and tongues which were present in the Early Church are for us
today, if they would also accept the practice of selling all their
possessions and give all of it away for the help of others? Was
this community project of selling all and pooling it together one
which should be practiced today? We already saw in Acts 2
that the early Christians sold their possessions and here we read
that "no one said that anything of what he possessed was his
own." In consequence of having all things in common, want
and poverty should have been unknown among them. This will
be the rule in the Kingdom when Christ reigns on earth, and of
course the apostles were still dreaming of this. While this practice lasted it certainly was a great testimony to the Jews in
Jerusalem.

But as the Gospel went to the Gentiles the practice was abandoned. It lasted but for a brief period, and we find no mention of it again. It does not work in this dispensation. On
Gentile ground we find no such conditions. The practice of
selling all was entirely voluntary. It was not a command, and
it operated only while the Church was small and limited to
Jerusalem. Chapter 4 closes with the account of Barnabas
voluntarily giving all his possessions for the work of the Gospel,
and being blessed for it. But the impracticability of the custom
soon becomes evident, for the very next chapter tells of the
abuse of the practice by Ananias and Sapphira, and the chapter
after that records the murmuring of certain ones who did not get
their proper share.

But . . .

After the sweet picture of love which we have seen, the picture
is soon marred, and the next chapter (Acts 5) opens with a
great big *but!* It is in sharp contrast to the happy scene of the
assembly having all things in common. All was peace and

harmony as we closed chapter four of Acts, and then a *but! But!* And with this little word, "but," the story of evil and discord begins. Satan had been unable to dim the testimony of the disciples from the outside by persecution. Seeing that outside attacks only made the disciples stronger, he now enters within the little flock, and begins his work *within* the assembly. This is an old trick of the Devil. When he cannot destroy the work of the Church by attacking from the outside world, he will work from within and use the members within the assembly to break up the testimony. All he needs is one or two "members" of the family to start a rumpus, and soon the whole thing explodes from within. I am not half as fearful of the most vicious enemies of the Church in the outside world as I am of one pious member in the Church who has "gone sour" and is out of fellowship. He can do more to hinder and wreck the testimony than all the attacks from without.

In our story, the Devil used two people (very pious people) to mar the happy scene. They were Ananias and Sapphira. The story begins with *but!*

> But a certain man named Ananias, with Sapphira his wife, sold a possession,
> And kept back part of the price, his wife also being privy to it, and brought a certain part, and laid it at the apostles' feet (Acts 5:1, 2).

They wanted to put on a very pious front, and would not be outdone by Barnabas and his magnanimous gift of all his possessions. But it was voluntary. No one was under obligation to do the same. Th motive of Ananias and Sapphira was the exact opposite of that of Barnabas. Moved by deceit, they lied about the transaction, for they pretended to give the *entire price* of the sale, whereas they held back a part of it for themselves. The evil was not in retaining part of the price, but in telling a lie about it. Peter detects the deception, and says:

> . . . Ananias, why hath Satan filled thine heart to lie to the Holy Ghost, and to keep back part of the price of the land?
> Whiles it remained, was it not thine own? and after it was sold, was it not [still] in thine own power? . . . (Acts 5:3, 4).

At these words of Peter, God struck Ananias down and he died, as did his wife later when she repeated her husband's lie. This is the last we hear about the practice of "sharing" all things alike. It did not work as long as there were some who did not go along with it. In the Kingdom Age when all God's people are willing to do this, there will be no problem, for it will mean equal distribution for all, and undoubtedly then those who practice deceit will also be struck down even as Ananias and Sapphira. In the next chapter we shall see how the apostles tried to meet the abuse of this system by the appointment of the seven men to look after the distribution of the funds. You must recognize from this that we cannot take everything that the Early Church did, as a pattern or rule for our practice today. All this was still in Jerusalem. All this was before a single Gentile had been added to the Church. All this was still on Kingdom ground. If you feel that the practice of selling all and giving it to others is for today, go ahead, brother, and try it. No one will object. Start it off and see how it works. How necessary it is to "rightly divide the word of truth."

MIRACLES, SIGNS, HEALINGS

The same principle applies to the verses which immediately follow the account of Ananias and Sapphira:

> And by the hands of the apostles were many signs and wonders wrought among the people; . . .
>
> Insomuch that they brought forth the sick into the streets, and laid them on beds and couches, that at the least the shadow of Peter passing by might overshadow some of them.
>
> There came also a multitude out of the cities round about unto Jerusalem, bringing sick folks and them which were vexed with unclean spirits: and they were healed *every one* (Acts 5:12, 15, 16).

Every one! No failures, no one was sent home unhealed "because they did not have faith." These miracles were apostolic signs for Israel. The scene was still Jerusalem. How is it that people today take this in support of present healing movements? If the healing the apostles wrought in this passage is claimed, then it must be possible by a shadow to heal folks in their beds and *it must never fail.* In the apostolic gifts of healing there were no *failures.* Every one the apostles chose to heal was *healed. Every one!* No dodging here, no excuses; they were healed *every one.* Apply this test to the popular healing ministries (so-called) of today.

The result was electrifying! The rulers placed the disciples in the common prison. But the angel of the Lord opened the prison doors and when the officers came the next day to bring them to trial, they were gone. When they were found, they were right back at it again — in the Temple proclaiming the message of the crucified, risen Christ. They are still in Jerusalem, and their message is still to the nation of Israel. Once again they are brought before the council and asked why they were disobedient to the command of the religious court. Peter had the answer:

> . . . We ought to obey God rather than men (Acts 5:29).

And then he boldly launches upon his testimony for Christ once more, and makes it personal:

> The God of our fathers raised up Jesus, whom ye [speaking to the nation] slew and hanged on a tree (Acts 5:30).

This was too much, and they began to plan the destruction of the apostles. But there was one man in the council, Gamaliel by name, who convinced them not to resort to violent means to stop the disciples. As a result they abandoned their plans to kill the apostles, and after beating them and commanding them to cease preaching they let them go. The chapter closes with a great testimony to the faith of these disciples, for in spite of the threatenings of the Sanhedrin, we read:

> And daily in the temple, and in every house, they ceased not to teach and preach Jesus Christ (Acts 5:42).

However, the Devil does not leave Christians alone when they are really on fire for God, and so Acts 6 opens with a scene of discord, dissatisfaction and murmuring. Pressures from the outside only drove the disciples closer together, and the greater the persecution from the enemies on the outside world, the more vigorous their testimony and zealous their endeavors. Satan knows the effectiveness of the destruction which can be wrought by strife within the family. You can explode a whole case of dynamite on top of a rock without doing much more damage than making a noise, but bore a hole into the heart of the rock and insert only one stick of dynamite, and you can blow that rock to "smithereens."

Surely here in the Early Church we have recorded a warning against the wiles of the enemy. In our next message we shall take up the cause of the dissension in the Early Church as recorded in Acts 6. May we suggest before reading the next chapter, that you carefully read the first seven verses in Acts 6. As we study the subtle entrance of carnality and sin into the happy family of the Early Church, we are reminded of the words of Peter:

> Be sober, be vigilant; because your adversary the devil, as a roaring lion, walketh about, seeking whom he may devour (I Peter 5:8).

CHAPTER NINE

The First Christian Martyr

The sixth chapter of Acts opens with a scene of trouble, dissension and murmuring, and ends with a scene of persecution. It opens with a complaint of certain members of the erstwhile peaceful congregation in Jerusalem:

> And in those days, when the number of the disciples was multiplied, there arose a murmuring of the Grecians against the Hebrews, because their widows were neglected in the daily ministration (Acts 6:1).

Trouble was brewing in the First Church in Jerusalem. It was the result of the communal practice of pooling their possessions and distributing them among the members. Many of the disciples sold all they possessed, and gave it to the apostles to be distributed by them among the poorer members. The Jews usually had a fund in the Temple for just such situations, but these Christians were, of course, not eligible for this help. This custom may have had something to do with the practice in the Early Church. But the practice had its weaknesses. We saw the tragic misuse of it in the case of Ananias and Sapphira. Now in this chapter the apostles were charged and accused of favoritism. The foreign-born, Greek-speaking Jews complained that they were being neglected. Their widows did not receive the same apportionment of the community funds. These widows belonged to a group of foreign-born Hebrews. They are called Grecians (Hellenists) because they spoke Greek and were not born in Judea. The apostles who were the custodians and trustees of the community funds were accused of favoring the home-born Hebrews and neglecting these foreign-born Jews.

The apostles therefore suggested that they be relieved of this responsibility, and offered a solution:

> Then the twelve called the multitude of the disciples unto them, and said, . . .
>
> . . . look ye out among you seven men of honest report, full of the Holy Ghost and wisdom, whom we may appoint over this business.
>
> But we [the apostles] will give ourselves continually to prayer, and to the ministry of the word (Acts 6:2-4).

The suggestion was well received, and seven men, usually referred to as the first deacons were chosen. Their names were Stephen, Philip, Prochorus, Nicanor, Timon, Parmenas and Nicolas, a proselyte of Antioch. It is interesting to note in passing that all these names are Greek names, so that the Grecian Jews could not accuse the apostles of appointing *biased* or *prejudiced* stewards. These seven "deacons" were charged with distributing to and helping the poor. They had nothing to do with running the Church, but were to be interested only in the material needs of the people. The Greek word *diakonos* means literally "an errand boy."

Two of the deacons, however, were more than errand boys and had a higher purpose than merely being helpers for the apostles. These two deacons were Stephen who became the first Christian martyr, and Philip, who after the martyrdom of Stephen in Jerusalem, went to preach the Gospel in Samaria.

The First Martyr

With the introduction of this man Stephen we reach a critical stage, an important turning point in the book of Acts. You will recall the commission of Jesus was: (1) in Jerusalem and Judaea; (2) into Samaria; and (3) unto the uttermost part of the earth (Acts 1:8). With the stoning of Stephen we come to the close of the first stage — Jerusalem and Judaea. Up until now the testimony of the apostles had been given only to Jews and only in the city of Jerusalem. This stage, "to the Jew first," is now to be closed, and the deacon Stephen is the instrument chosen by God to bring the final testimony to the nation of Israel. Immediately after his stoning, we have the message going into Samaria (Acts 8), and the second stage is begun. The record of

this important stage and crisis and turning point in Acts begins
in chapter 6, verse 8,

> And Stephen, full of faith and power, did great wonders
> and miracles among the people.
> Then there arose certain of the synagogue, . . . disputing
> with Stephen.
> And they were not able to resist the wisdom and the spirit
> by which he spake (Acts 6:8-10).

Now remember this was still in Jerusalem. Stephen's ministry
was to the Jews in Jerusalem. He is addressing the nation of
Israel, but the reaction to Stephen's preaching was violent.

> Then they suborned men, [induced them to lie] which said,
> We have heard him speak blasphemous words against Moses,
> and against God.
> And they stirred up the people, . . . and brought him to
> the council,
> And set up false witnesses, which said, This man ceaseth
> not to speak blasphemous words against this holy place [the
> temple], and the law:
> For we have heard him say, that this Jesus of Nazareth
> shall destroy this place, and shall change the customs which
> Moses delivered us.
> And all that sat in the council, looking stedfastly on him,
> saw his face as it had been the face of an angel (Acts 6:11-15).

There should be no chapter division between Acts 6 and 7.
There should be no break, for Acts 7 is a direct continuation
of chapter 6:

> Then said the high priest, Are these things so? (Acts 7:1).

Before going further, notice that Stephen is before the highest
tribunal of the nation of Israel, the Sanhedrin, presided over by
the high priest. Stephen's defense is before the nation officially
as represented by the high court of the Sanhedrin. He therefore
addresses them as follows:

> . . . Men, brethren, and fathers, hearken; The God of
> glory appeared unto our father Abraham, when he was in
> Mesopotamia, before he dwelt in Charran (Acts 7:2).

The rest of this chapter is devoted by Stephen to a recitation
of the history of the nation. We suggest you read the entire
record in this chapter. It is familiar, and we will not take the
space to deal with it here. We move right on to the conclusion

of Stephen's message and the reaction of the council. Having finished his review of Israel's history, he now makes his application. It is the last offer of the Kingdom to Israel:

> Ye stiffnecked and uncircumcised in heart and ears, ye do always resist the Holy Ghost: as your fathers did, so do ye.
>
> Which of the prophets have not your fathers persecuted? and they have slain them which shewed before of the coming of the Just One; of whom ye have been now the betrayers and murderers:
>
> Who have received the law by the disposition of angels, and have not kept it (Acts 7:51-53).

This was too much for the enemies of Stephen, and

> . . . they were cut to the heart, and they gnashed on him with their teeth.
>
> But he, being full of the Holy Ghost, looked up stedfastly into heaven, and saw the glory of God, and Jesus *standing* on the right hand of God,
>
> And said, Behold, I see the heavens opened, and the Son of man *standing on the right hand of God* (Acts 7:54-56).

The critical moment has come. Once more the Lord through Stephen offers to set up the Kingdom, restore the nation and deliver Israel upon condition of repentance. They had rejected it when it was preached by John the Baptist and by the disciples of Jesus. They had rejected it when Peter made the offer at Pentecost, and now for the final time the offer is made. Stephen sees the Messiah of Israel *standing up in heaven*. When our Lord ascended into Heaven, He *sat down* at the right hand of God the Father (Hebrews 1:3; Hebrews 10:12). But here He is *standing up* before an opened door in Heaven. The meaning should be clear. Their Messiah is ready to return, if Israel will repent at this invitation by Stephen. But instead, they reject the offer, the door in Heaven is closed, and Jesus sits down again to await the time when, after the Church is gone, they will "look upon Him whom they had pierced" and be converted. God foreknew this rejection, in order that He might bring in, during the days of Israel's setting aside, the Church which is His Body.

THE MURDER OF STEPHEN

Upon the conclusion of Stephen's testimony and the vision of the open Heaven and Messiah standing ready to return, the mob rushes upon him:

> Then they cried out with a loud voice, and stopped their
> ears, and ran upon him with one accord,
>
> And cast him out of the city, and stoned him: and the wit-
> nesses laid down their clothes at a young man's feet, whose
> name was Saul.
>
> And they stoned Stephen, calling upon God, and saying,
> Lord Jesus, receive my spirit.
>
> And he kneeled down, and cried with a loud voice, Lord,
> lay not this sin to their charge. And when he had said this,
> he fell asleep (Acts 7:57-60).

This concludes the first part of the program of Christ, as
commissioned to His disciples — "beginning at Jerusalem." It
has now gone to the Jew first, and we are ready to enter upon
the second step in the program — *into Samaria*. Before recording
the ministry of Philip in Samaria, we have an introduction to
a new personality who is to take over the stage in the last chapter of Acts. His name is Saul. He was present at the martyrdom
of Stephen, consenting in his death, and was the custodian of the
clothes of those who stoned Stephen.

> And Saul was consenting unto his [Stephen's] death. And
> at that time there was a great persecution against the church
> which was at Jerusalem; and they were all scattered abroad
> throughout the regions of Judaea and Samaria, except the
> apostles.
>
> As for Saul, he made havock of the church, entering into
> every house, and haling men and women committed them
> to prison (Acts 8:1, 3).

Paul is now to be the instrument for the carrying out of the
third stage of the program, "unto the uttermost part of the
earth."

The Lord now turns from Jerusalem and the nation. They
had their chance, and the time is come to bring the Gospel to
others. Saul, still unsaved, was God's instrument to accomplish
this, for it was because of Saul's persecution of the Christians
in Jerusalem that,

> . . . they were all scattered abroad throughout the regions
> of Judaea and Samaria (Acts 8:1).
>
> Therefore they that were scattered abroad went everywhere
> preaching the word (Acts 8:4).

God moves in a mysterious way. The Apostle Paul, the apostle to the Gentiles, was used by God, even before he was saved, to bring about the spreading of the Word by the scattering of the persecuted saints in Jerusalem.

THEN PHILIP WENT

Before the conversion of Saul is recorded (Acts 9) and he goes on his missionary journey to the Gentiles (Acts 13) we are introduced to Philip the deacon. After the stoning of Stephen by the leaders of the nation, and the scattering of the persecuted disciples, the record continues:

> *Then* Philip went down to the city of Samaria, and preached Christ unto them (Acts 8:5).

This is the first time the Gospel goes beyond Jerusalem and Judaea. It is the first time it is brought to any others but the Jews at Jerusalem. "To the Jew first" is now history. And unlike the ones to whom the message came in Jerusalem, here in Samaria the message is gladly received.

> And the people with one accord gave heed unto those things which Philip spake, hearing and seeing the miracles which he did.
>
> For unclean spirits, crying with loud voice, came out of many that were possessed with them: and many taken with palsies, and that were lame, were healed.
>
> And there was great joy in that city (Acts 8:6-8).

How thankful we should be that in God's eternal program He has included us and not the members of one nation only. Although God chose one nation to be the vehicle for giving us the revelation of Himself, and the channel through which not only the Messiah of Israel but also the Saviour of the world was to come, yet He is Saviour of all.

Today there is no excuse for anyone having heard this message to still be lost. In the providence of God the Gospel is going out into all the world. Maybe someone has never really heard the simple story, so we repeat it once more. You are a sinner by birth and under condemnation. You are helpless to save yourself, but God sent His Son to die on the cross for your sins, raised Him from the dead to prove that sin had been put away, and now offers you by simple faith, salvation full and free. "Whosoever will may come."

CHAPTER TEN
The Keys of the Kingdom

The order in which the Gospel was to be preached after the day of Pentecost was first *in Jerusalem and all Judaea;* then *in Samaria,* and then *unto the uttermost part of the earth* (Acts 1:8). The book of Acts is the record of the carrying out of this program. Stage number one, first to the Jews in Jerusalem and Judaea, begins in chapter 1 and closes with the stoning of Stephen in chapter 7. Then follows step number two, and Philip is chosen to bring the message to Samaria. After the persecution following Stephen's death the disciples were scattered abroad and the message goes beyond Judaea. And now we come to an important section of the book:

> Now when the apostles which were at Jerusalem heard that Samaria had received the word of God, they sent unto them Peter and John:
> Who, when they were come down, prayed for them, that they might receive the Holy Ghost:
> (For as yet he was fallen upon none of them: only they were baptized in the name of the Lord Jesus.)
> Then laid they their hands on them, and they received the Holy Ghost (Acts 8:14-17).

This is the first time the apostles had left Jerusalem. Up until now the Gospel was preached only to Israel and the ministry was confined to Jews only. But now it had gone beyond Judaea to Samaria and so Peter and John were sent to these believers in Samaria. We ask the question, Why was Peter sent to Samaria? Why could not Philip lay hands on these believers so they could also receive the Holy Ghost which was poured out at Pentecost on the Jerusalem company? Misunderstanding of the reason for this has led to all kinds of confusion. This was not a second outpouring of the Holy Spirit upon the Samaritans. The Holy Spirit had been poured out "once for all" at Pentecost on the body of believers. Now the Samaritans were also to be received into that body and made to share in the Pentecostal baptism of the Holy Spirit. When Peter and John laid hands on these Samaritans, they did not experience the *baptism* of the Spirit, but they *received* the Holy Spirit. They were made partakers of the Holy Spirit which had already fallen upon the Church in Jerusalem. But why did Peter have to come to bring this about? The answer lies in the commission Jesus had given Peter as the bearer of the keys of the Kingdom. Peter was chosen to open the door of the Gospel. Upon the confession of Peter that Jesus was the Christ (Matthew 16:16), the Lord said to him:

> And I will give unto thee the keys of the kingdom of heaven: and whatsoever thou shalt bind on earth shall be bound in heaven: and whatsoever thou shalt loose on earth shall be loosed in heaven (Matthew 16:19).

What were these keys? Did Peter have the power to save people or forgive their sins? Would we dare to trust our salvation to a vacillating, fallible, stumbling Peter? God pity those who do. The keys Christ gave to Peter were three in number: one to open the door of the Gospel to the Jews in Jerusalem, one to open the door to the Samaritans in Samaria (Acts 8); and one to open the door to the Gentiles in the house of Cornelius, the first Gentile converts (Acts 10). This was the first time Peter used the keys committed to him. He fades completely out of the picture, and Paul the apostle to the Gentiles takes over. All this was in perfect accord with the program Christ commanded in three stages: first, Jerusalem; second, Samaria; third, to the Gentiles. In each case it was Peter who was the instrument to open the Gospel door. In each case it resulted in their receiving the Holy Spirit. As the program was in these three steps: Jews, Samaritans, Gentiles; so Pentecost came first on the believers in Jerusalem, was extended to those in Samaria, and finally also to the Gentiles in Caesarea. In the case at Jerusalem it was accompanied by a mighty wind, tongues of fire, and speaking in the various languages of the world. When the Samaritans received the Holy Spirit there is no mention of wind or fire or any speaking in tongues. In the case of Cornelius, there is speaking in tongues, but no wind and no fire. Three different manifestations of the same outpouring Spirit. If we claim this same experience today, which one of these shall we choose, for they were all different.

But I hear someone object and say, "You said there was only one Pentecost, never to be repeated in this church age, and now you mention three: Jerusalem, Samaria and Caesarea." Pardon me, we did not mention *three* Pentecosts, but that *one* Pentecost was manifested on three occasions to conform with the commission, "beginning at Jerusalem, Samaria, and the uttermost parts of the earth." To help you understand this, we turn to the first mention of Pentecost in the Scriptures. It is found way back in Leviticus 23, and it will give us the key to the interpretation in the book of Acts. Pentecost was the fourth feast in order, following (1) The passover; (2) unleavened bread; and (3) firstfruits. The Passover was a type of the death of Christ; the unleavened bread typifies His burial; and the firstfruits His resurrection. Fifty days after the firstfruits (resurrection) came Pentecost.

> And ye shall count unto you from the morrow *after* the sabbath [Sunday] . . .
> Even unto the morrow after the seventh sabbath shall ye number fifty days; and ye shall offer a new meat offering unto the LORD (Leviticus 23:15, 16).

This was the feast of Pentecost called here "fifty days," the literal translation of the word "Pentecost." In Deuteronomy 16, Pentecost is also referred to as a feast of weeks and the time of harvest. Pentecost began the harvest season and the Lord gave definite instructions concerning this harvest in three separate stages. Carefully study this verse in concluding God's command for the observance of Pentecost (Leviticus 23:22).

> And when ye reap the harvest of·your land [beginning at Pentecost], thou shalt not make clean riddance of the corners of thy field when thou reapest, neither shalt thou gather any gleaning of thy harvest: thou shalt leave them unto the poor, and to the stranger: I am the LORD your God (Leviticus 23:22).

Notice carefully, there are three parts to this reaping: (1) The main body of the harvest; (2) the corners of the field; (3) the gleanings of the harvest. And these three parts of the harvest

festival were for three classes of people; first, for the owners of
the land; then next, for the poor; and finally, for the strangers
within their gates. The owners and first partakers are Israel;
next come the poor, the Samaritans; and finally the strangers,
the Gentiles. But all three parts and all three classes were
included in the one harvest of Pentecost, one Pentecostal
outpouring of the Holy Spirit upon the three classes mentioned
by Jesus beginning at Jerusalem, and Samaria, and to the uttermost parts of the earth. The keys entrusted to Peter were to un-
lock the treasures of the Holy Spirit to these three groups, ending the use of the keys dispensationally, and Peter's work is
done and he disappears from the scene. We repeat there is a
wide difference in the manifestation of the receiving of the Holy
Spirit in these different stages. Which of the three patterns
shall we follow if we insist on another outpouring of the Holy
Spirit? Shall we follow the pattern of the Jews in Jerusalem, the
Samaritans in Samaria, or the Gentiles in Caesarea?

Before leaving this subject we would remind you of the forward
and backward look of Pentecost. Before that day came, Jesus
promised it as future. He said,

> For John truly baptized with water; but ye shall be bap-
> tized with the Holy Ghost not many days hence (Acts 1:5).

Jesus did not say you will be baptized *many times* for many
days in the future. He said it would happen *not many days
hence*. When Jesus said this, it was still future. About twenty-
five years later Paul said it was past — it was history.

> For by one Spirit are [have] we all [been] baptized into
> one body, whether we be Jews or Gentiles . . . (I Corinthians
> 12:13).

Notice when Jesus gave the promise of the baptism it was
future. Twenty-five years later Paul says it is past. Somewhere
between it had come, and of course we know it was at Pentecost. Acts 1:5 points forward to Pentecost; it was prophecy.
But twenty-five years later, it was history. At what point did the
prophecy of the baptism in the Spirit become history? The
answer is Acts *two!*

We return now to the eighth chapter of Acts. After Peter's
use of the keys in opening the Gospel to the Samaritans and their
receiving the Holy Spirit, we have the story of Simon the sor-

cerer who wanted to buy this apostolic power with money. We suggest you read the account in Acts 8:18-24. We pass on to the return of the apostles to Jerusalem. The keys had been used and they return to Jerusalem awaiting the call to the final use of the keys in Acts 10.

> And they [Peter and John,] when they had testified and preached the word of the Lord, returned to Jerusalem, and preached the gospel in many villages of the Samaritans (Acts 8:25).

New Door Opens

Now a new door opens and the message can go even beyond the limits of Samaria unto the uttermost parts of the earth. Philip's ministry in Samaria is terminated by the coming of Peter, and he is sent to a wider ministry.

> And the angel of the Lord spake unto Philip, saying, Arise, and go toward the south unto the way that goeth down from Jerusalem unto Gaza, which is desert.
>
> And he arose and went: and, behold, a man of Ethiopia, an eunuch of great authority under Candace queen of the Ethiopians, who . . . had come to Jerusalem for to worship,
>
> Was returning, and sitting in his chariot read Esaias the prophet (Acts 8:26-28).

This eunuch was probably a Gentile, possibly a proselyte to Judaism. Philip's preaching to this "stranger" and "outcast" to the commonwealth of Israel, anticipates and introduces the third and last stage of Jesus' commission, "unto the uttermost part of the earth."

Philip meets this stranger in the desert, is invited to come and sit in the chariot with this man who was reading the fifty-third chapter of Isaiah. But he could not understand who this servant of Jehovah was, and so he asks Philip:

> . . . of whom speaketh the prophet this? . . . (Acts 8:34).

This was Philip's chance and he preached the Gospel to this man, and this man, Gentile or proselyte, was gloriously saved, and was baptized by the side of the road. It is a picture of the program for this age. The Gospel is no more limited to Jews only, or Samaria, but for those also who are afar off. Here the order is believe, confess, be baptized. Saved by believing, manifested by confession and testified to by baptism. And after the Gospel had symbolically gone to the uttermost part of the earth, something surprising happens.

Philip Is Caught Away

And when they were come up out of the water, the Spirit
of the Lord caught away Philip, that the eunuch saw him no
more: and he went on his way rejoicing (Acts 8:39).

Literally the expression "caught away" is *raptured*. The word
translated "caught away" occurs no less than eleven times in the
New Testament. The word is *harpazo* and is translated
"caught up" in II Corinthians 12:2, where Paul was caught up
into the third Heaven. The same word is used in I Thessa-
lonians 4:17 concerning the Rapture of the Church:

Then we which are alive and remain shall be *caught up*
together with them in clouds. . . .

The "catching away" of Philip after leading the eunuch to
Christ is a picture of the *rapture* — catching away of the Church
after the Lord has called out from among the Gentiles a people
for His Name. Philip may be taken to represent the Church,
which in the beginning witnessed to Israel, then to the Samaritans and then to all nations (as represented by the eunuch), and
when that number is full, the Church (like Philip) will be raptured and taken to another place, the house of many mansions
now being prepared for us.

That glorious day is drawing near. The ministry of the Church
is moving toward its climax when the last believer foreordained
by God is added to the Body of Christ; and then the Spirit of
the Lord will catch the Bride away, and usher in earth's greatest
time of trial, to be climaxed by earth's greatest day of peace,
prosperity and plenty. One of these days the Church, represented by Philip, will hear the call, "come up hither."

For the Lord himself shall descend from heaven with a
shout, with the voice of the archangel, and with the trump
of God: and the dead in Christ shall rise first:

Then we which are alive and remain shall be caught up
together with them in the clouds, to meet the Lord in the
air: and so shall we ever be with the Lord.

Wherefore comfort one another with these words (I Thes-
salonians 4:16-18).

CHAPTER ELEVEN
To the Jew First

The ninth chapter of the book of Acts records the greatest and most important event in the entire book, with the exception of the second chapter which relates the outpouring of the Holy Spirit on Pentecost. It contains the conversion account of Saul who later became Paul.

> And Saul, yet breathing out threatenings and slaughter against the disciples of the Lord, went unto the high priest,
> And desired of him letters to Damascus to the synagogues, that if he found any of this way [Christians], whether they were men or women, he might bring them bound unto Jerusalem (Acts 9:1, 2).

We first meet Saul at the stoning of Stephen in chapter 7. Here he was consenting to the death of Stephen, and was custodian of the clothes of the executors. He became the leader in a great persecution of the Christians in Jerusalem with the result that the disciples (except the apostles) were driven out of Jerusalem and scattered far and wide. One of these was Philip, the deacon evangelist, who was the first to carry the gospel message beyond the limits of Judaea.

The Three Steps Again

We repeat here once again the program laid down by the Lord just before His ascension. He said in Acts 1:8,

> . . . ye shall be witnesses unto me both in Jerusalem, and in all Judaea, and in Samaria, and unto the uttermost part of the earth (Acts 1:8).

The first stage of this program ended with the stoning of Stephen; the second stage is recorded in chapter 8; and the third and last stage properly begins with the conversion of Saul, the apostle to the Gentiles, in chapter 9. During the three years Paul spent in Arabia being prepared for his ministry, we have the closing activities of Peter in Acts 10 to 12. In the 13th chapter the first missionaries are sent beyond the limits of the land of Palestine. Before studying the details of his dramatic conversion on the road to Damascus, we introduce you to the man Saul before his conversion.

Saul was a Jew (he calls himself a "Hebrew of the Hebrews"). He was born in Tarsus, the capital of Cilicia, and the home of one of the greatest universities of philosophy in that day. He was a member of the sect of the Pharisees, and also a member of the highest ruling body in Israel, the Sanhedrin. Saul was an intensely religious man, zealous for the cause of Judaism, and a sworn enemy of the new sect known as Christians. He was a man of high moral character and he describes himself in Philippians 3:

> Circumcised the eighth day, of the stock of Israel, of the tribe of Benjamin, an Hebrew of the Hebrews; as touching the law, a Pharisee;
> Concerning zeal, persecuting the church; touching the righteousness which is in the law, blameless (Philippians 3:5, 6).

Paul was a highly educated scholar, trained in the city of Jerusalem, at the feet of Gamaliel, one of the greatest Jewish religious teachers of that day. He says in Acts 22,

> I am verily a man which am a Jew, born in Tarsus, a city in Cilicia, yet brought up in this city [Jerusalem] at the feet of Gamaliel, and taught according to the perfect manner of the law of the fathers, and was zealous toward God, as ye all are this day (Acts 22:3).

Paul was not a criminal, a drunk or a down-and-outer. He was a highly respected, polished, cultured, law-abiding, religious man. We stress this point because of his dramatic, sudden and explosive conversion. There are many people who believe that sudden and dramatic conversions are for the down-and-outer, the bum or the criminal. Thousands of people believe that folks who have lived good, moral lives, trained in a religious atmosphere, brought up in the church and taught the doctrines of the Bible, do not need a conversion experience. They were born in a Christian home, trained in the church, joined the church, and lived decent, moral lives, and therefore they have always been Christians and need not have a conversion experience. To this mistaken idea we can point to two outstanding men whose experiences totally contradict these false notions. The one is Nicodemus, a fine, moral, religious, educated, earnest, exemplary citizen, and yet Jesus said to this man, *ye must be born again.* The other man is Saul, on whose moral character could be found no spot, and whose religious zeal was honest and sincere, but he found all this of no avail when he met Christ face to face. In Philippians 3 he says that after he was converted, "he counted all things as refuse." We are now ready to look at this meeting of this exemplary religious Hebrew with the Lord Jesus Christ. While Saul was on the way to Damascus with warrants for the arrest of Christians,

> . . . suddenly there shined round about him a light from heaven:
> And he fell to the earth, and heard a voice saying unto him, Saul, Saul, why persecutest thou me?
> And he said, Who art thou, Lord? And the Lord said, I am Jesus whom thou persecutest: it is hard for thee to kick against the pricks.
> And he trembling and astonished said, Lord, what wilt thou have me to do? And the Lord said unto him, Arise, and go into the city, and it shall be told thee what thou must do (Acts 9:3-6).

It is impossible to go into all the detailed teaching and applications of Paul's conversion. We suggest that the reader study it carefully for himself. There are, however, a few important highlights which deserve special attention. One of the first things to notice is the rapidity of the spread of Christianity, due to the zeal and determination of the scattered disciples. Until the stoning of Stephen, the preaching of the Christians had been confined to Jerusalem. With the persecutions led by Saul following Stephen's death, the disciples were scattered and had gone as far as Damascus. It could hardly have been more than a year since they were driven out of Jerusalem, and yet enough believers had been won to Christ to draw the attention of Saul to that city. Truly the blood of the martyrs is the seed of the Church, and days of persecution are far more spiritually productive than days of undisturbed peace. These believers were still meeting in the Jewish synagogues and this must have irritated Saul and his cohorts greatly. So they set out to arrest the Christians for profaning the sacred precincts of the synagogue.

The second significant thing about Paul's conversion was the supernatural manner. Now every conversion is, of course, a supernatural act, but in the case of Paul it was accompanied by a number of supernatural manifestations in the natural realm. There was a light from Heaven, and an audible voice speaking from Heaven. It was accompanied by a physical shock which threw Paul to the ground. Unbelievers and skeptics try to tell us Paul suffered from sunstroke or had an attack of epilepsy, but the account which follows shows how ludicrous and absurd are the attempts of the natural man to explain the supernatural. Notice next that this appearance of Jesus to Paul was one of only three instances after Pentecost when Christ revealed Himself from Heaven. The first one to see the ascended Lord was Stephen in Acts 7:56. Then he was seen and heard by Saul who beheld him in that glory brighter than the noonday sun (I Corinthians 15:8). The last time the glorified Christ manifested Himself was to John on the island of Patmos (Revelation 19:11). These three appearings after the ascension coincide to the three aspects of His Second Coming. First He will appear to His waiting Church, represented by Stephen. This speaks of the Rapture. Then He will appear to Israel, represented by the conversion of Saul. Saul, a zealous, religious Jew, is converted, and becomes the witness and testimony to the whole world. Thus the nation of Israel (typified by Saul) will "look upon Him whom they have pierced," will behold Him in the Tribulation and be saved. And then finally He will appear as John saw Him at Patmos, as the One who comes to judge the earth and set up His long-promised millennial Kingdom.

One other thought we must mention in the conversion of Saul. Jesus identifies Himself with the people Saul was seeking to destroy. The voice from Heaven said, "Saul, Saul, why persecutest thou *me?*" That was indeed strange, for Paul was persecuting the Christians at Damascus. His wrath was against the Church, but Jesus says, "You are persecuting *me!*" Christ as the Head, and the Church as His Body, are *one,* and what Paul was doing against the Christians, he was doing against Jesus Himself. No wonder Paul asks, "Who art thou, Lord?" Notice that Paul recognizes the voice as the voice of God. He calls Him "Lord," and then comes the great surprise, for the answer is, "I am Jesus." This Jesus whom he despised and hated, and whose followers he was persecuting, was God, the Lord in whose name he was seeking to destroy the Christians. And now notice very, very carefully, that Paul immediately acknowledged the deity of Jesus. He sees now that Jesus was God and immediately replies, "Lord (God) what wilt thou have me to do?" This was to be the new message from now on, "Believe that Jesus is the son of God." This was the message to the Philippian jailor, to Lydia, and to all his hearers on his missionary journeys, "Believe on the *Lord* Jesus Christ." After his confession of Jesus as Lord he arose from the earth, but found he was totally blind. His associates had to lead him by the hand to a house in Damascus on Straight Street, where a man named Judas kept him in his home for three days.

MINISTRY OF ANANIAS

Paul had put himself in the hands of the Lord, and now the Lord undertakes for him. The Lord speaks to a certain disciple with orders to go visit Paul. The Lord gave this disciple Paul's street address, so that he could find him. The Lord said unto Ananias:

> . . . Arise, and go into the street which is called Straight, and enquire in the house of Judas for one called Saul, of Tarsus: for, behold, he prayeth (Acts 9:11).

At first Ananias was afraid, and says:

> . . . Lord, I have heard by many of this man, how much evil he hath done to thy saints at Jerusalem:
> And here he hath authority from the chief priests to bind all that call on thy name (Acts 9:13, 14).

But the Lord tells Ananias he need not be afraid. He tells him he has already informed Saul that he (Ananias) was coming over and was already in prayer (Acts 9:11, 12). Then the Lord assures Ananias, and says,

> . . . Go thy way: for he [Saul] is a chosen vessel unto me, to bear my name before the Gentiles, and kings, and the children of Israel:
> For I will shew him how great things he must suffer for my name's sake (Acts 9:15, 16).

Inexhaustible are the lessons contained in this brief passage. Time would fail us completely to point out all the precious personal applications we can make of these passages. We mention just a few:

1. God knows the exact address of all His children. He knows the street number of each and every one. When He spoke to Ananias he gave him the street address where Paul was staying.

2. God makes preparation for our need beforehand. When blindness smote Saul, He already had an Ananias to come to help with him.

3. When the Lord saves a person, He also prepares a work for him. We are saved to serve. The Lord not only saves us to keep us out of hell and take us to Heaven when we die, but for every person the Lord saves, He has a job.

That was the message Ananias was to tell to the new convert, Saul. You are "a chosen vessel unto me, to bear my name before the Gentiles, and kings, and the children of Israel."

4. There is a fourth application we want to make. Young converts need the help of older Christians. God spoke to an older Christian to go and minister to a babe in Christ. How precious the record:

> And Ananias went his way, and entered into the house; and putting his hands on him said, Brother Saul, the Lord, even Jesus, that appeared unto thee in the way as thou camest, hath sent me, that thou mightest receive thy sight, and be filled with the Holy Ghost.
>
> And immediately there fell from his eyes as it had been scales: and he received sight forthwith, and arose, and was baptized.
>
> And when he had received meat, he was strengthened. Then was Saul certain days with the disciples which were at Damascus (Acts 9:17-19).

The conversion of Saul introduces the third stage of the commission of our Lord; (1) Jerusalem; (2) Samaria; (3) Gentiles. Paul's conversion was miraculous but it was not a repetition of Pentecost. After Paul was saved he was baptized. Notice carefully. Paul first was saved by receiving the Lord on the road to Damascus. Next the blindness of Paul was ended by the coming of Ananias. Then Paul was filled with the Holy Ghost. This was not a *baptism* in the Holy Spirit, but a *filling*. There is no record that Paul began to speak in tongues or had some ecstatic experience when he was filled with the Spirit.

Then, after he had (1) believed, and (2) received his sight, he was (3) filled with the Holy Spirit and was baptized. Baptism did not precede Paul's salvation, nor did it precede his being filled with the Holy Spirit, but followed all these, merely as a testimony. The order is the same today. The first requisite is to *believe*. Paul was saved at his meeting with the resurrected Saviour. He confessed Him as Lord and was saved. It is still so:

> That if thou shalt confess with thy mouth the Lord Jesus, and shalt believe in thine heart that God hath raised him from the dead, thou shalt be saved (Romans 10:9).

CHAPTER TWELVE

The World's Greatest Missionary

After the conversion of Saul on the road to Damascus, he went back to school for three years. Although he had received his education, both secular and religious, in the best educational institutions of his day, he needed more than a secular and religious education before he could set out on his life work as the greatest missionary of all time. He therefore spent three years somewhere in Arabia, receiving firsthand instruction by special revelation from Heaven in preparation for his missionary work and the writing of his inspired epistles. We do not know the details of Paul's journey to Arabia. We know only the bare facts. He mentions it clearly in Galatians:

> But when it pleased God, who separated me from my mother's womb, and called me by his grace,
> To reveal his Son in me, that I might preach him among the heathen; immediately I conferred not with flesh and blood:
> Neither went I up to Jerusalem to them which were apostles before me; but I went into Arabia, and returned again unto Damascus.
> Then after three years I went up to Jerusalem to see Peter, and abode with him fifteen days (Galatians 1:15-18).

ORDER OF EVENTS

This order of events is related in Acts 9:20-27. After Saul was brought to Damascus and filled with the Spirit, he began to witness immediately.

> And straightway he preached Christ in the synagogues, that he is the Son of God (Acts 9:20).

Paul lost no time but began to witness in the very synagogues where he was intending to arrest and bind the Christian believers. No wonder they were amazed and filled with doubt, fearing that this was only a ruse to find out their identity. But Paul continued to witness. We do not know for how long, but after his brief stay in Damascus he left for Arabia for three years. His stay in Arabia is shrouded in mystery, but we believe it fits in between the 22nd and 23rd verses of Acts 9:

> But Saul increased the more in strength, and confounded the Jews which dwelt at Damascus, proving that this is very Christ (Acts 9:22).

The next verse begins with the phrase, "And after that many days." This is quite likely a reference to the many days of three years he spent in Arabia. Then after these "many days" he returns to Damascus and resumes his testimony among the Jews in the synagogue. But his message was not received, and

> . . . the Jews took counsel to kill him:
> But their laying await was known of Saul. And they watched the gates day and night to kill him.
> Then the disciples took him by night, and let him down by the wall in a basket (Acts 9:23-25).

Having been rescued from the plot of his enemies and under cover lowered over the wall in a basket, he now sets out for Jerusalem. Three years and more have passed since his conversion, and this is his first visit to the apostles in Jerusalem. Most of the three years he spent in Arabia receiving special revelation concerning the Church, about which the apostles in Jerusalem as yet knew nothing. They were still expecting the setting up of the Kingdom. The truth of the Church, the body of Christ during this dispensation, was still much of a mystery to the apostles in Jerusalem. But Paul had received a new revelation which was not too readily received by the apostles at the first. During his stay in Arabia he was caught up into Heaven, and heard and saw things never revealed before. We have the record in II Corinthians 12, where Paul tells us of this experience. He says,

> . . . that he was caught up into paradise, and heard unspeakable words, which it is not lawful for a man to utter (II Corinthians 12:4).

Whatever the revelation Paul received directly from Heaven may have been, it was something entirely new. The apostles in

Jerusalem were unable to tell Paul anything he had not already
received. After his three years in the Seminary of the Holy
Spirit, he went to visit Peter in Jerusalem, *not* to receive any
instructions from the apostles, for he had a divine ordination.
He did not go to Jerusalem to be officially ordained an apostle
by the "First Church in Jerusalem." No official body had authority in Jerusalem to pass upon Paul's ordination or ministry.
No church council, no meeting of a presbytery or synod received Paul, but he saw only Peter and James. During Paul's
visit to Jerusalem, he was under deep suspicion by the apostles,
as to his official call as an apostle. They suspected Paul of being
a spy, and only after the intervention of Barnabas did they
tolerate him. The Christians in Jerusalem

> . . . were all afraid of him, and believed not that he was
> a disciple.
> But Barnabas took him, and brought him to the apostles,
> and declared unto them how he had seen the Lord in the way,
> and that he had spoken to him and how he had preached
> boldly at Damascus in the name of Jesus.
> And he was with them coming in and going out at
> Jerusalem.
> And he spake boldly in the name of the Lord Jesus, and
> disputed against the Grecians (Grecian Jews): but they
> were about to slay him (Acts 9:26-29).

To save Paul from his enemies at Jerusalem, his friends took
him to Caesarea, and from there to his hometown, Tarsus.

PETER'S FINAL MINISTRY

Here in Tarsus Paul spent some time waiting for the official
opening of the door to the Gentiles by Peter, before embarking
on his first missionary journey. In the meantime Peter is to make
his final appearance on the scene. The balance of Acts 9, therefore, is an account of Peter's ministry, while Paul is being prepared to take the spotlight in the rest of the book of Acts.
Peter's ministry to Jerusalem and Judaea and Samaria is first
to be concluded. So while Paul is waiting in Tarsus, Peter travels
to Lydda and heals a man by the name of Aeneas who had been
paralyzed for eight years. From there he goes to Joppa on the
seacoast. In the city of Joppa a certain disciple named Dorcas
took sick and died. Knowing that Peter was in Lydda and
probably having heard of the healing of Aeneas, they sent for

Peter to come to Joppa, a distance of only about ten miles from Lydda. Here Peter raises Dorcas from the dead. Remember all this was still in Judaea. Peter had not yet gone beyond the confines of the second stage of Christ's commission, "beginning at Jerusalem, and all Judaea, and Samaria." After the raising of Dorcas, Peter remains in Joppa. The closing verse of Acts 9 is tremendously significant:

> And it came to pass, that he [Peter] tarried many days in Joppa with one Simon a tanner (Acts 9:43).

There is no mention of any preaching or any other activity by Peter for many days in Joppa. He was detained there by the Holy Spirit in preparation for the next important event in the book of Acts; viz., the opening of the door of the Gospel to the Gentiles. This we find in the next chapter (Acts 10). To Peter had been committed the keys of the Kingdom. He, as the leader of the apostles, was to be God's instrument in opening the door in harmony with Jesus' commission *first* in Jerusalem; second, in Samaria; and finally, "the uttermost part of the earth;" viz., the Gentiles. He had exercised the use of the keys in Jerusalem on the day of Pentecost. This was the first key, "to the Jews first." Then he had exercised the second key when he was called to open the door in Samaria (Acts 8:14-17). Now, before the third stage (to the Gentiles) is to begin, Peter must use the keys once more for the last time in the house of the Gentile Cornelius, as related in Acts 10.

But Peter had to be prepared first for this drastic departure from the "kingdom" program. Peter did not yet believe the Gospel was for the Gentiles. He still believed it was limited to the house of Israel, and for any Gentile to be saved, he must become a Jew, submit to circumcision and place himself under the laws of Moses. Peter was yet to learn that the middle wall of partition between Jew and Gentile had been broken down and that in Christ there is neither Jew nor Gentile, neither bond nor free. Peter was a devout Israelite. To him the Gentile was an unclean dog with whom he could have little in common. The first indication of the great lesson Peter was to learn, before he could accept Gentiles on the same plane as himself, was begun by the Lord, when Peter was led to lodge in the house of Simon.

A Tanner

Simon was a tanner by occupation, which made necessary the handling of skins and hides of unclean animals. It was a trade considered unclean by the devout Israelite. We see in this the first step in the Lord's dealing with Peter to open the door of the Gospel to the unclean Gentiles in the house of Cornelius. But before Peter is to go on this revolutionary and unheard-of mission, the Holy Spirit prepares the way. He prepares the heart of a Gentile, Cornelius, to receive the Word, while at the same time he prepares his divinely appointed instrument, Peter, to bring the message, contrary to all the traditions and practices of the past. First he prepares the heart of Cornelius:

> There was a certain man in Caesarea called Cornelius, a centurion of the band called the Italian band.
>
> A devout man, and one that feared God with all his house, which gave much alms to the people, and prayed to God alway (Acts 10:1, 2).

This man was a Gentile and lived in a Gentile city. He was an officer in the Gentile Roman army. He served the despised government of Rome who oppressed and ruled over the proud nation of Israel in their own covenant land. This man, however, was a sincere, religious man. He was devout, feared God, prayed much and was liberal with his possessions. But he evidently was *not* saved. He was sincerely religious, but lost. I realize there are those who believe that Cornelius was already saved before Peter came. We would not argue the point as it is relatively unimportant. The thing to notice is that it is the work of the Holy Spirit to begin the work of salvation in men's hearts. Salvation is a sovereign act of God in grace, choosing His own elect and providing that the means of their salvation, the spoken Word, shall be made available to them. The vision of Cornelius and his instruction to send for Peter was the work of the Holy Spirit in his heart. But when Peter rehearses the experience later to the disciples in Jerusalem he makes it quite clear that Cornelius and his company were *not* saved until after Peter had preached to them, and they had believed. No other construction can be placed on Peter's words in Acts 11:14. The angel said to Cornelius,

> . . . Send men to Joppa, and call for Simon, whose surname is Peter;

> Who shall tell thee words, whereby thou and all thy house
> *shall* be saved (Acts 11:13, 14).

Notice the words, *shall be saved.* They were saved by believing the message of Peter. It points up the important truth that being religious is not salvation. Paul himself was fanatically religious, but unsaved. Nicodemus was unimpeachably religious, but he was not saved. Cornelius was a wonderful man, religiously and morally, but spiritually dead. The message of the angel to Cornelius was:

> . . . send men to Joppa, and call for one Simon, whose surname is Peter:
> . . . he shall tell thee what thou oughtest to do (Acts 10:5, 6).

This was an act of sovereign grace. The Lord did not choose to save Cornelius because he was such a fine religious man; the work was the work of the Holy Spirit. But we must also add that Cornelius obeyed the Word of the Lord to him. And so we read:

> And when the angel . . . was departed, he called two of his household servants, . . .
> And . . . sent them to Joppa (Acts 10:7, 8).

The salvation of Cornelius was an act of sovereign grace, but it also depended upon the response of Cornelius. It brings us face to face with the mystery of the sovereign grace of God and the responsibility of man. God does the choosing and the electing and the foreordaining, but at the same time man must do the believing. This mystery we cannot understand. It is true that only those who are elected of God will be saved. It is equally true that we must *believe* in order to be saved. I repeat, this is a mystery only God understands. It is not ours to argue about, or to explain or understand. It is ours to accept and believe.

Again and again we hear the argument, "If God does the electing, then it is true that only those whom God elects will be saved." This we cannot deny if we believe in the unquestioned sovereignty of God. But it is equally true that those who are elect will also believe. Understand this? Of course not! We would have to be as wise as God to understand this apparent paradox. Let me therefore ask you, "Would you really like to know whether you are one og God's elect?" Be sincere now, and stop trying to understand it, and answer the question, "Would you like to be sure you are one of God's elect?" Then listen — stop arguing and accept God's invitation, "Come unto Me, and I will give you rest." *Believe on the Lord Jesus Christ, and thou shalt be saved. Whosoever shall call upon the name of the Lord shall be saved.* God does the electing; you must do the believing, and if you are really serious, then right now accept His promise, "Him that cometh to me, I will in no wise cast out" (John 6:37). Election is God's business; believing is your business. Do your part, and you may know you are one of His own. Jesus combines the great truth of God's part and our part in one concise verse:

All that the Father giveth me *shall come* to me . . . (John 6:37).

That is God's part, but notice the rest of the verse:

. . . and him that cometh to me, I will in no wise cast out (John 6:37).

That is your part! Will you come?

CHAPTER THIRTEEN

Sovereign Grace in Action

In the Old Testament there were only two classes of people in the sight of God. These were Jews and Gentiles. The nation of Israel was God's chosen covenant nation. They were the physical descendants of Abraham through Isaac and then through Jacob. They consisted of the twelve tribes of Israel. All outside this nation were Gentiles. To become participants of God's covenant promises, these Gentiles must become Jews, proselytes to the religion of Israel, submit to circumcision and place themselves under the laws of Moses. But all this was changed when Christ came, and was rejected by His people. While the nation is temporarily set aside because of this rejection of their Messiah and King, the Lord is calling out a third company in this dispensation, called the Church and the body of Christ. This consists of all who have received Christ by faith. In this body there are no racial or national distinctions or barriers. All are one in Christ Jesus. We can do no better than to quote the words of Paul in Ephesians addressed to the Gentile members of the Church:

> Wherefore remember, that ye being in time past Gentiles in the flesh, who are called Uncircumcision by that which is called the Circumcision in the flesh made by hands;
>
> That at that time ye were without Christ, being aliens from the commonwealth of Israel, and strangers from the covenants of promise, having no hope, and without God in the world (Ephesians 2:11, 12).

This was the status of every Gentile outside Israel. They were outcasts, considered unclean and were referred to as dogs

(Matthew 15:26). However, by the death and resurrection of Christ all this is changed and a new body of persons comes into view, and so Paul continues:

But now in Christ Jesus ye [Gentiles] who sometimes were far off [separated] are made nigh by the blood of Christ.

For he is our peace, who hath made both one [believing Jews and Gentiles], and hath broken down the middle wall of partition between us;

Having abolished in his flesh the enmity, even the law of commandments contained in ordinances; for to make in himself of twain *one new man,* so making peace;

And that he might reconcile both unto God [both Jews and Gentiles] in one body by the cross, having slain the enmity thereby:

And came and preached peace to you [Gentiles] which were afar off, and to them [Jews] that were nigh.

For through him we both [Jews and Gentiles] have access by one Spirit unto the Father (Ephesians 2:13-18).

This was the new message of Pentecost, specially revealed to the Apostle Paul. However, this revolutionary Gospel was not readily received by the apostles at first, steeped as they were in the traditions of their racial superiority. Now turning again to Acts 10, we see how the Lord prepared the Apostle Peter for this new revelation. We left Peter at Joppa in the house of Simon the tanner. His next assignment was to Caesarea to use the keys of the Kingdom of Heaven in opening the door to the Gentiles in the house of Cornelius. But Peter was hardly ready for this turn of events. He still believed that the Gospel was for Israel, and for a Gentile to be saved he must be circumcised, place himself under the law and become a Jew.

The Heavenly Vision

The Lord had already prepared the heart of the Gentile Cornelius to receive the Gospel. Now Peter must be prepared as the bearer of the keys to preach it to them. It was quite unthinkable for Peter to go to a Gentile, let alone an officer in the Roman army who was oppressing his people the Jews. The Lord had a wonderful way of teaching Peter his new assignment. While the messengers from Cornelius were on their way, Peter (still in Joppa) went up on the housetop for his midday devotions. He became extremely hungry and ordered some food, but then fell into a trance:

> And saw heaven opened, and a certain vessel descending unto him, as it had been a great sheet knit at the four corners, and let down to the earth:
> Wherein were all manner of fourfooted beasts of the earth, and wild beasts, and creeping things, and fowls of the air.
> And there came a voice to him, Rise, Peter; kill, and eat.
> But Peter said, Not so, Lord; for I have never eaten any thing that is common or unclean (Acts 10:11-14).

Peter emphatically protests this command to eat of this Heaven-sent food. In this sheet from Heaven were all manner of unclean animals strictly forbidden under the law of Moses to Israel. He was able to say he had been a strict law-keeper. And so Peter refused the command, but the voice came the second time, and added:

> . . . What God hath cleansed, that call not thou common [unclean] (Acts 10:15).

Then a third time came the command to eat things forbidden as unclean under the law. Then Peter awoke and was really confused. What could this mean? Under the law Peter was strictly forbidden to eat unclean foods (Leviticus 11). And here the same Lord who forbade eating these foods, now commands Peter to eat. Does God contradict Himself, or did God change His mind? It was all so confusing. It is just another example of the need of rightly dividing the Word of truth. This seeming contradiction can only be explained dispensationally. Under the dispensation of the law, Israel was forbidden many things and commanded to do many things which do not apply today to this dispensation of grace. Israel was commanded to keep the seven feast days, to destroy their enemies and burn their cities. All these laws were given to keep Israel separate from the Gentiles about them. The restriction concerning unclean foods was to prevent social intercourse between the Israelites and the Gentiles. The orthodox Jew could not accept an invitation to dinner with a Gentile because these unclean foods would be served. Israel must be kept segregated in order to fulfill God's purposes through them.

But now God has set Israel aside for a time, and is calling out from all nations a Church, a body of believers who under

grace would not be in bondage to the law of Moses. Jews and
Gentiles in this body of this dispensation are united in one.
They are one, and the restricting laws which separated Jew
and Gentile are done away in Christ. On the cross Christ fulfilled all the demands of the law of which Paul says that He
blotted

> . . . out the handwriting of ordinances that was against
> us, which was contrary to us, and took it out of the way,
> nailing it to his cross;
>
> Let no man therefore judge you in meat, or in drink, or
> in respect of an holyday, or of the new moon, or of the sab-
> bath days:
>
> Which are a shadow of things to come [the law]; but the
> body is of Christ (Colossians 2:14, 16, 17).

No, the Bible does not contradict itself. Where it seems to be
a contradiction, it is failure to interpret the passages dispensationally and to "rightly divide the word of truth." What was
commanded under the law was not necessarily so under *grace*.

PETER'S LESSON

This lesson Peter had to learn before he was ready to go to
the Gentile house of Cornelius. No wonder he was confused.
But he was soon to find out. The answer came in an unexpected
visit of a company of men.

> Now while Peter doubted in himself what this vision
> which he had seen should mean, behold, the men which
> were sent from Cornelius had made enquiry for Simon's
> house, and stood before the gate,
>
> And called, and asked whether Simon, which was sur-
> named Peter, were lodged there.
>
> While Peter thought on the vision, the Spirit said unto
> him, Behold, three men seek thee.
>
> Arise therefore, and get thee down, and go with them,
> doubting nothing: for I have sent them (Acts 10:17-20).

Peter meets the men and is informed that God had also
spoken to the Gentile Cornelius, and told him to send for Peter.
Now the light begins to dawn upon Peter, and the vision of the
sheet begins to take on meaning. God had said, "What I have
cleansed, call thou not common." Next morning Peter goes
with the men to Caesarea. Cornelius had gathered his family
and relatives and friends, a great congregation of *Gentiles*.

When Peter arrived, Cornelius fell down to worship Peter; horrified, Peter lifted him up and said, "Stand up. I myself also am a man." Peter would not permit men to bow and kneel before him, or give him any special honor.

Seeing the crowd, and realizing this thing was of God, he begins to understand the meaning of the sheet which came down from Heaven filled with both clean and unclean animals. Listen to Peter's opening words. He had to explain how it was that an orthodox Israelite should enter into the house of a Gentile:

> And he said unto them, Ye know how that it is an *unlawful* thing for a man that is a Jew to keep company, or come unto one of another nation; but God hath shewed me that I should not call any man common or unclean [Peter now understands the message of the sheet].
>
> Therefore came I unto you without gainsaying [without objection], as soon as I was sent for: I ask therefore for what intent ye have sent for me? (Acts 10:28, 29).

Then Cornelius tells how he had received a message from Heaven to send for him, and that there should be no misunderstanding, the angel gave the name and the city and the address of Simon Peter. All doubts are gone now, and Peter preaches the Gospel to them — the same story of the death and the resurrection of Jesus. The mystery of the great sheet full of animals is all cleared up at last. There is far more here than merely the privilege under grace of eating foods heretofore forbidden to Israel. To be sure, this is here. We are not under the dietary restrictions of the Old Testament, but live in the liberty of grace. That application is merely incidental. The real lesson Peter had to learn was a dispensational lesson. It was the passing of the age of Law, and the coming of the dispensation of the Grace of God. This is to be a new body consisting of both Jews and Gentiles who receive and acknowledge the Lord Jesus Christ.

THE SHEET IS THE CHURCH

The great sheet which Peter saw is a picture of the Church of this dispensation. We may take the four corners as the four of the earth to which this *whosoever* Gospel was to go. It is the carrying out of the third phase of our Lord's commission, "unto the uttermost part of the earth." The clean animals in the sheet represented the Jews, and the unclean animals represent the

Gentiles. By the grace of God these too are cleansed as Paul says to the Corinthian Gentiles,

> . . . but ye are washed, but ye are sanctified, but ye are justified in the name of the Lord Jesus, and by the Spirit of our God (I Corinthians 6:11).

One more thing we want to point out. This sheet came down from Heaven, and it went back to Heaven. The sheet we believe represents the Church which had its origin in Heaven; chosen in Christ from eternity, it was born on the day of Pentecost by the baptism in the Heaven-sent Holy Spirit. The Church is a Heavenly people as Israel is God's earthly people. This distinction people had to learn, that the Church born on the day of Pentecost was to be the Bridegroom's bride in Heaven, while Israel is to be more closely associated with the Millennial Kingdom on earth.

But as the origin of the Church in the sheet was Heaven, so the destiny of the Church is also Heaven. The beginnings of the Church, the day of Pentecost, is over nineteen hundred years in the past. We cannot help but discern the signs of the return of Christ. While the time is unknown, the fact is beyond question. Paul leaves no doubt in our minds when He assures us that,

> . . . the Lord himself shall descend from heaven with a shout, with the voice of the archangel, and with the trump of God: and the dead in Christ shall rise first:
>
> Then we which are alive and remain shall be caught up together with them in the clouds, to meet the Lord in the air: and so shall we ever be with the Lord.
>
> Wherefore comfort one another with these words (I Thessalonians 4:16-18).

The most pressing question for each one personally is, "Do I belong to that Body represented by the sheet in Peter's vision?" You can settle it today.

CHAPTER FOURTEEN

Peter's Last Use of the Keys

How wonderful the grace of God! What a transforming power it is — able to change a persecutor of the Church into the great apostle of the Gentiles, the Apostle Paul. Or think of the Apostle Peter, a law-abiding, zealous Jew, going to the Gentile house of Cornelius in Caesarea to preach the Gospel of the grace of God. We have the account of Peter's first sermon to a Gentile congregation in Acts 10:

> Then Peter opened his mouth, and said, Of a truth I perceive that God is no respecter of persons:
> But in every nation he that feareth him, and worketh righteousness, is accepted with him (Acts 10:34, 35).

Imagine Peter saying, "God is no respecter of persons." Where did he get this notion? Previously Peter had looked upon God as a respecter of persons and had raised objections to his going to preach to the Gentiles, so God had to show him by the vision of a sheet filled with clean and unclean animals. Peter was now convinced that the Gospel was also for the Gentiles. Cornelius and his family had heard about Jesus but thought of Him only as Israel's Messiah, and now Peter informs them that He is the Saviour of all men. He says,

> The word which God sent unto the children of Israel, preaching peace by Jesus Christ: (he is Lord of all:)
> That word, I say, ye know, which was published throughout all Judaea, and began from Galilee, after the baptism which John preached (Acts 10:36, 37).

This message of the Kingdom, preached by John and the apostles, they had heard about, but they did not know the Gospel of the grace of God for all nations. That message Peter now brings to the household of Cornelius and he ends his message with the words,

> To him give all the prophets witness, that through his name *whosoever believeth* in him shall receive remission of sins (Acts 10:43).

This was a new message. It was not the message Peter had preached at Pentecost. This message to the Gentile Cornelius differs from the message to Israel in at least four important aspects:

1. Peter's message at Pentecost was addressed exclusively to the Jews at Jerusalem, while here it is not only to the Gentile Cornelius, but it is *whosoever believeth* in Him shall receive remission of sins.

2. Peter in his message to Israel quotes to them from the Old Testament to show that Jesus was the promised Messiah foretold by the prophets. In his sermon to Cornelius he does not mention the Old Testament but confines his message to the death and resurrection of Jesus.

3. In Peter's message to Israel the emphasis is on *repentance,* while in his message to Cornelius he never once mentions repentance, but the important word is *believe.* This does not mean that Gentiles do not have to repent. Repentance is an indispensable requirement in salvation, but the emphasis is on personal faith rather than national repentance. Of course, there can be no true repentance without faith, nor can there be true faith without repentance. But at Pentecost it was national repentance which was required. In the house of Cornelius it was *personal faith.*

4. At Pentecost, water baptism preceded the receiving of the Holy Spirit; but here in Caesarea, baptism follows the receiving of the Holy Spirit. Water baptism is not a requirement for salvation, but a testimony of a salvation already received. It is not a means of grace, it is not a sacrament. But Peter recognizes the value of the rite of baptism as a testimony of identification with the death and burial of Christ, and so he says, after the family of Cornelius was saved,

> Can any man forbid water, that these should not be baptized, which have received the Holy Ghost as well as we? (Acts 10:47).

The conversion of these Gentiles was in response to hearing the Word as preached by Peter. In reality Peter never even finished his sermon, for it was interrupted before he was through. Notice verse 44:

> While Peter yet spake these words, the Holy Ghost fell on all them which heard the word.
>
> And they of the circumcision [Jews] which believed were astonished, as many as came with Peter, because that on the Gentiles also was poured out the gift of the Holy Ghost.
>
> For they heard them speak with tongues, and magnify God (Acts 10:44-46).

Great confusion has resulted from a misunderstanding of this initial experience of receiving the Holy Spirit in the family of Cornelius. This was not another outpouring of the Spirit, but here the Gentiles become partakers of the *one* baptism of Pentecost. We have already seen that the Samaritans received the same gift. In all three instances it was on the occasion of Peter's use of the keys. First when Jerusalem received the baptism in the Spirit (Acts 2), it was Peter who brought the message. In Samaria Peter again used the keys to open the Gospel to the Samaritans (Acts 8), and they became partakers of the Pentecostal experience. And now the third and last use of the keys is accompanied by the Holy Spirit receiving the Gentiles into the Body.

DIFFERENT MANIFESTATIONS

In none of the three incidents of the Gospel going to Jews, Samaritans and Gentiles, was the experience the same. At Pentecost the Spirit was manifested by a mighty wind and tongues like as of fire. In Samaria the Holy Spirit was received by the laying on of the hands of the apostles. There is no baptism mentioned and no speaking in tongues. However, in the case of the Gentiles the Spirit came in response to the hearing of the Word. There was no laying on of hands, no wind or fire, but here speaking in tongues did follow. Here are three different circumstances where Jews, Samaritans and Gentiles received the Holy Spirit, and they were all different. Which shall we follow, if these are meant for us today?

Why Tongues Among Gentiles?

Here we must answer an oft repeated question. If tongues are not for us Gentile believers today, how then do we explain why these Gentile converts in the house of Cornelius *did* speak in tongues? The answer will become evident. This was the *first* time the Gentiles are received into the Body of Christ. To demonstrate to the Jewish believers that the Gospel is now also to go to the Gentiles, they were made to speak in tongues. It was the evidence to the Jews that these Gentiles too were represented in the Pentecostal blessing of Acts 2. Notice the words, when these Jews saw the Gentiles receiving the Spirit:

> And they of the circumcision [Jews] which believed were astonished, as many as came with Peter [six of them], because that on the Gentiles also was poured out the gift of the Holy Ghost (Acts 10:45).

And the evidence to these Jews was the fact that they heard them speak with tongues. It was not an easy matter to prove to these Jewish disciples from Jerusalem that these strangers in Caesarea had been admitted into the Body, and they needed some proof as seen in the manifestation of tongues. The sign of tongues was given because of their *unbelief*. Paul also explains this in I Corinthians 14:22,

> Wherefore tongues are for a *sign, not to them that believe,* but to them that *believe not.*

There were many in the church of Corinth who would not believe except they saw signs and wonders. They were weaklings in the faith, babes in Christ, and the Lord accommodates Himself by stooping to give these weak believers an additional sign, a sort of a crutch to help them learn to walk by faith. The tongues in the home of Cornelius were likewise a sign to the Jews who needed this evidence that Gentiles also were included in the blessing of Pentecost. Paul says, "For the Jews require a sign, and the Greeks seek after wisdom: But we preach Christ crucified, . . . the power of God, and the wisdom of God" (I Corinthians 1:22-24).

At Pentecost the tongues were all among the members of Israel. In the case of Cornelius, the sign of tongues was again for the benefit of the Jewish believers who had come with Peter (Acts 10:45). The correctness of this interpretation is made plain in the next chapter:

> And the apostles and brethren that were in Judaea heard
> that the Gentiles had also received the word of God.
>
> And when Peter was come up to Jerusalem, they that were
> of the circumcision contended with him.
>
> Saying, Thou wentest in to men uncircumcised, and didst
> eat with them (Acts 11:1-3).

PETER CALLED TO GIVE ACCOUNT

As soon as Peter arrives in Jerusalem he is called on the carpet for his actions in the house of Cornelius. He is severely criticized for his very unorthodox behavior in fellowshiping with Gentiles, and Peter was forced to defend himself, which he did most effectually:

> But Peter rehearsed the matter from the beginning, and
> expounded it by order unto them, saying,
>
> I was in the city of Joppa praying: and in a trance I saw a
> vision, A certain vessel descend, as it had been a great sheet,
> let down from heaven by four corners; and it came even to me:
>
> Upon the which when I had fastened mine eyes, I considered, and saw fourfooted beasts of the earth, and wild
> beasts, and creeping things, and fowls of the air.
>
> And I heard a voice saying unto me, Arise, Peter; slay
> and eat (Acts 11:4-7).

Then Peter rehearses at length the thrice-repeated command, and how the messengers from Cornelius had come to the house seeking him. He tells how he went with them, and then clinches it all by telling how these Gentiles also received the gift of the Holy Ghost. Peter concludes his argument with the convincing words:

> Forasmuch then as God gave them the like gift as he did
> unto us, who believed on the Lord Jesus Christ; what was
> I, that I could withstand God? (Acts 11:17).

Peter's testimony was convincing. He had exercised the use of the keys in opening the Gospel to the Gentiles, and

> When they heard these things, they held their peace, and
> glorified God, saying, Then hath God also to the Gentiles
> granted repentance unto life (Acts 11:18).

The tongues were for the Jews to convince them of the acceptance of the Gentiles into the Body.

A STRANGE PARADOX

The door to the Gentiles was now open. The disciples in Jerusalem admitted this, *but* it was not with an entirely willing heart. They could not gainsay Peter's testimony but they themselves wanted to be excused. While convinced that the Gentiles could be saved, they still held on to their own prejudices and dislike for these uncircumcised heathen, and would not offer the Gospel to them. This indeed was a strange situation. They had accepted Peter's word about the conversion of the household of Cornelius, but as far as these Judaistic Christians were concerned, it ought to stop with this one family, and go no farther. Hence we read in the very next verse (verse 19):

> Now they which were scattered abroad upon the persecution that arose about Stephen travelled as far as Phenice, and Cyprus, and Antioch, preaching the word *to none but unto the Jews only.*

They still could not accept the Gentiles, and confined their preaching strictly to Jews only. However, in their journey they were accompanied and joined by believers from Cyprus and Cyrene who kicked over the traces and began preaching to the Grecians in the city of Antioch. The results were amazing,

> And the hand of the Lord was with them: and a great number believed, and turned unto the Lord (Acts 11:21).

A great revival broke out in Antioch among the Gentiles and large numbers were saved. It caused such a stir that the news of the revival soon reached the ears of the disciples in the "First Christian Church" in Jerusalem. It was cause for great alarm and action must be taken immediately. Luke records it as follows:

> Then tidings of these things came unto the ears of the church which was in Jerusalem: and they sent forth Barnabas, that he should go as far as Antioch.
>
> Who, when he came, and had seen the grace of God, was glad, and exhorted them all, that with purpose of heart they would cleave unto the Lord (Acts 11:22, 23).

Barnabas had been sent by the elders of the Jerusalem Church to report what was going on in Antioch, but when he saw what God was doing he did *not* return to Jerusalem, but instead hurried to Tarsus to get Saul to come to Antioch. Barnabas knew the lingering bigotry and aversion to the Gentiles which still lurked in the hearts of the Christians in Jerusalem. Barnabas knew the die-hard prejudices which would seek to put out the revival fires in Antioch, and so instead of going back to Jerusalem he hurries on to get Saul. We shall take up the story from here in our next chapter.

Let us speak of one or two practical observations in closing. Bigotry and prejudices are sin. The Jerusalem Christians could not be happy about the revival in Antioch because it did not originate with them. Who had authorized these evangelists from Cyprus and Cyrene to preach in Antioch, and of all things to the Gentiles? This is a subtle sin all too prevalent today. Can we rejoice in a revival in another church besides our own? Can we see beyond our church and denomination? Can we rejoice when God gives another preacher a more fruitful ministry than He gives us? Do we pray for only *our* church, *our* denomination, *our* missionaries? Do we support only *our* little program, or do we have a vision beyond the narrow limits of our own sectarian group? May we with John learn to say,

He must increase, but I must decrease (John 3:30).

CHAPTER FIFTEEN

God's Care for His Own

"The blood of the martyrs is the seed of the Church." This has been true in the history of the Church of Jesus Christ. Times of prosperity and freedom from opposition and oppression have always been days of spiritual decline and decay, while the days of the severest persecution have been the times of greatest revival and growth. It was so from the very beginning. During the early days of the Church following Pentecost, the Devil tried his best to destroy Christianity, but it only resulted in its spread. While trying to stamp out the fire, it only scattered the sparks far and wide, and burst into flame on every hand. We have seen this in the persecutions which followed the martyrdom of Stephen, the deacon. In Acts 11:19, 21 we read:

> Now they which were scattered abroad upon the persecution that arose about Stephen travelled as far as Phenice, and Cyprus, and Antioch . . .
> And the hand of the Lord was with them: and a great number believed, and turned unto the Lord.

Notice carefully this revival was *not* in Jerusalem. It did not even originate in Jerusalem, but in Antioch. The Gospel had gone to Jerusalem first, to Israel, but now it is to go to the Gentiles, and the scene now shifts from Jerusalem to Antioch. From now on Antioch becomes the center of Gospel preaching. The first missionaries are to be sent from Antioch — not Jerusalem. Antioch, not Jerusalem, now becomes the headquarters of the Church. And simultaneously with this, Peter the apostle of the circumcision bows out of the picture, and Paul the apostle to the Gentiles takes over. All this is prophetic. The Gospel had

gone to the Jew first. The Kingdom was offered to the nation
of Israel, but they had rejected their Messiah *in Jerusalem*.
Now the nation is set aside and the Church enters upon the
stage, and so the scene shifts from the capital of Israel, Jerusalem, to the Gentile city of Antioch. God is through with Jerusalem
and Israel for the time being, and is dealing now with the
Church, the Body of Christ.

REVIVAL IN ANTIOCH

The attention of the Church is first drawn to Antioch because
of a mighty revival which broke out as the result of the preaching of certain evangelists from Cyprus and Cyrene. When the
news reached the apostles in Jerusalem, they sent Barnabas to
investigate. But instead of returning to Jerusalem, knowing the
deep-seated prejudices among the disciples there, he goes to
Tarsus and brings back Saul to continue with him the work
so signally blessed in Antioch (Acts 11:25). They remained
in Antioch a whole year. And here in Antioch the believers
were first called Christians. It was, however, not meant as a
compliment, but a nickname of contempt. They called these
believers Christians, or in modern parlance "Christites" — followers of the despised Christ. However, though it was meant
as a derisive name, it was the greatest compliment which could
possibly be given the believers at Antioch.

RESULT OF THE REVIVAL

The closing verses of Acts 11 give us the fruit of the great
revival in Antioch. True revival is not a flash in the pan, a
few weeks of excitement, crowds and fanfare, but true revival
leaves behind it the fruits of the Spirit: love, joy and peace.
Thus it was in Antioch. The genuineness of the work of grace
in the hearts of the disciples in Antioch was manifested by their
ready help to their poor brethren in Jerusalem. A prophet named
Agabus predicted the coming of a great famine which would
leave the poor despised Christians in Jerusalem in great distress
(Acts 11:27, 28). These Jewish believers could not look to their
fellow Jews for relief, for they belonged to that despised company of believers in Christ. But the believers in Antioch came
to the rescue:

> Then the disciples, every man according to his ability,
> determined to send relief unto the brethren which dwelt in
> Judaea:

> Which also they did, and sent it to the elders by the hands
> of Barnabas and Saul (Acts 11:29, 30).

Just how long Saul and Barnabas remained in Jerusalem we do not know exactly, but during their stay a number of significant things take place. The second Christian martyr is slain (Acts 12:1, 2). Until this time, the persecution had been from the religious members of their own nation (Israel). Now Satan tries to exterminate the Christians by persecution from the political powers. Herod the king

> . . . killed James the brother of John with the sword
> (Acts 12:2).

When he

> . . . saw it pleased the Jews, he proceeded further to take
> Peter also . . .
>
> And when he had apprehended him, he put him in
> prison . . . (Acts 12:3, 4).

This is the third time Peter was put in prison, but again, he is marvelously delivered. The record of Peter's deliverance by the angel, the miraculous opening of the prison doors, and his arrival at the house of Mary the mother of John, where a prayer meeting in his behalf was in progress, are described in detail in this chapter (Acts 12). We rapidly pass over the well-known account, but suggest you read for yourself this interesting story (Acts 12:1-17). Imagine the surprise when the next morning Herod sent for Peter and found his cell empty.

> Now as soon as it was day, there was no small stir among
> the soldiers, what was become of Peter.
>
> And when Herod had sought for him, and found him not,
> he examined the keepers, and commanded that they should
> be put to death. And he [Herod humiliated and abashed]
> went down [like a coward] from Judaea to Caesarea, and
> there abode (Acts 12:18, 19).

This chapter closes with the judgment of God upon this wicked king who had killed James and persecuted the Christians. God will vindicate His own. Those who touch God's people touch the apple of His eye. We as believers do not have to vindicate ourselves against our enemies. We need not avenge ourselves, for God will avenge His own and vindicate His chosen ones.

No matter how severe the persecution, we can safely leave our persecutors in the hands of God who said:

> . . . Vengeance is mine; I will repay (Romans 12:19).

This is graphically illustrated in the judgment of God upon king Herod, the murderer of James.

> And upon a set day Herod, arrayed in royal apparel, sat upon his throne, and made an oration unto them [the people of Tyre and Sidon].
> And the people gave a shout, saying, It is the voice of a god, and not of a man.
> And immediately the angel of the Lord smote him, because he gave not God the glory: and he was eaten of worms, and gave up the ghost (Acts 12:21-23).

The Seed of the Church

Not only does God vindicate His own and avenge His elect, but He also turns tribulation into blessing, for in spite of the terrible persecution the Holy Spirit significantly adds, after the horrible death of Herod:

> But the word of God grew and multiplied (Acts 12:24).

During all this time Saul and Barnabas were in Jerusalem. They must have witnessed all these events, for they did not return to Antioch until after they had seen God's judgment upon the enemies of the Gospel. Surely this was to strengthen them for the task upon which they were to launch as soon as they returned to Antioch. In the days ahead when they too were persecuted and cast into prison, they must have remembered these incidents and encouraged themselves with the assurance that God would take care of His own in His own way and time. How much they needed this encouragement we shall soon see.

The First Foreign Missionaries

After the death of James and the imprisonment of Peter, Barnabas and Saul departed to go back to Antioch and took with them another disciple, John Mark. Their arrival in Antioch marks an important change in the program of the Early Church. In this chapter, the first foreign missionaries are sent out from the church at Antioch. The ministry of Peter comes to a close and we meet him only once again at the council in Jerusalem (Acts 15). The message of repentance to national Israel has been concluded, Peter disappears from view and the Apostle Paul takes over from here on. The final stage of the commission "unto all the world" is now to develop in earnest. The Gospel is now going to the Gentiles, but Paul did not overlook the fact that the Church was to consist of both Jews and Gentiles. So he usually went to the synagogue first when entering a city. It was the logical place to begin, for here he was assured of a hearing and an audience. However, the missionary journeys of Paul and Barnabas did not originate with the Jews in Jerusalem; they were not commissioned or sent forth by the apostles, and when they returned from that journey they did not go to report to the elders in Jerusalem, but they returned to the church at Antioch. The call to Israel, "to the Jew first," had been concluded, and now the Church which began at Pentecost with an "all Jewish" congregation, becomes predominantly Gentile. Hence the balance of Acts shifts from Jerusalem to Antioch. The scene opens in chapter 13:1,

> Now there were in the church that was at *Antioch* certain prophets and teachers; as Barnabas, and Simeon that was called Niger, and Lucius of Cyrene, and Manaen, which had been brought up with Herod the tetrarch, and Saul.
>
> As they ministered to the Lord, and fasted, the Holy Ghost said, Separate me Barnabas and Saul for the work whereunto I have called them.
>
> And when they had fasted and prayed, and laid their hands on them, they sent them away.
>
> So they, being sent forth by the Holy Ghost, departed unto Seleucia; and from thence they sailed to Cyprus (Acts 13:1-4).

Before following Barnabas and Saul on this pioneer missionary journey we must point out one or two things about the method in which these missionaries were called. While the happy assembly of believers in Antioch were praying and worshiping, the Holy Spirit spoke and said, "Set Barnabas and Saul apart for a special ministry." There were three others named (who also were prophets or teachers, or both), but the Holy Spirit singled out Barnabas and Saul for a specific ministry. Just how the Holy Spirit spoke and made known the will of the Lord in choosing these two men is not recorded. It may have been through one of the prophets in the assembly. During those days before the New Testament was written, God gave prophets to the Church

to make His will known. After the New Testament was complete
the gift of prophecy ceased, for there was no more need for it.
All we need to know to be assured of God's will for our lives
is in this Book. However, the Christians at Antioch had no New
Testament Scriptures and so God revealed Himself through
prophets, and by signs and wonders.

What method the Holy Spirit chose to designate Barnabas
and Saul is not the big question, for we believe it was made so
clear that there was no doubt in their minds. In this connection
we cannot help but recall how different it was in the days before
Pentecost. The disciples had been told to wait for the Holy
Spirit before they acted, but impetuous Peter could not wait,
and suggested a slate of candidates from which to choose a suc-
cessor to Judas. Instead of letting the Holy Spirit make the
choice and reveal His will as in the case of Saul and Barnabas
in Antioch, the flesh was listened to, and they had to *cast lots*
to decide whom to choose. There is quite a difference between
casting lots and allowing the Holy Spirit to make the choice.

The assembly at Antioch recognized the Spirit's call and
when they had fasted and prayed, they sent Saul and Barnabas
on their way. In the original it reads "and they let them go."
They did not send out these missionaries, but it was the Holy
Spirit who sent them forth, and they could only "let them go."
The very next verse guards against the notion that a church
can send out missionaries:

> So they, being sent forth by the Holy Ghost, departed
> . . . (Acts 13:4).

We sometimes wonder how many have been "sent out" by
men, by a church or by a missionary society, who were never
sent forth by the Holy Spirit. We make one other observation
before concluding this chapter. The whole procedure was one of
utmost simplicity. After the Holy Ghost had designated Barnabas and Saul as missionaries, they were not in a hurry, but resorted to some more fasting and praying. There were no for-
malities or fanfare. They formed no human plans, organized
no missionary board, appointed no committee, designated no as-
signed field. Assured that these men were called and sent forth
by the Holy Spirit, they were confident that He too would
provide for all their needs. All of it was in dependence upon the
guidance of the Spirit. How different our programs today!

What machinery, what organization and fleshly activity there is in so much of our program! In our present-day great movements (and if it isn't *big* it doesn't amount to anything), all we hear of in putting over the campaign or program is *men, money* and *methods*. Rallies, meetings, banquets and money-raising campaigns are resorted to, in order to stir up enthusiasm for the support of the program, and these are too often but an expression of self-reliance instead of dependence upon God.

How different the pattern in that first missionary conference in Antioch where Barnabas and Saul were sent forth. In the eyes of the world the simplicity of the whole account (comprehended in four short verses, Acts 13:1-4) did not seem like anything *big*, but it was the beginning of a movement that shook the world to its foundations.

In these days of mass production, fanfare and *big* things, may we recognize the importance of doing the seemingly obscure and unimportant things, remembering we are not called to success by the human standards of bigness or numbers or statistics, but only to be faithful to the call. We are so prone to be completely dazzled by the bigness of a thing rather than its usefulness and abiding value. We have lost the importance of the individual in the desire for a crowd. Yet Jesus came to save *individuals*.

CHAPTER SIXTEEN

Israel Today

"To the Jew first, and also to the Gentile." This was the order
in which the Gospel of the crucified, buried, risen Lord was to
be published (Romans 2:9, 19). This was the commission of
our Lord to His disciples on the day of His departure for Heaven.
It was His last order which He left them before He ascended.
We repeat it once more:

> But ye shall receive power, after that the Holy Ghost is
> come upon you: and ye shall be witnesses unto me both in
> Jerusalem, and in all Judaea, and in Samaria, and unto the
> uttermost part of the earth (Acts 1:8).

The first two stages of this threefold commission, Judaea and
Samaria, are history. The third stage, beginning in Acts 13,
is still going on and the Gospel is being proclaimed to the uttermost parts of the earth. The first part of the Lord's commission,
to the Jews in Judaea and the Samaritans (half-Jewish), was
committed to the apostles under the leadership of Peter and
Philip, the evangelist. As we come to Acts 13, Peter drops out
of the picture, for the ministry to national Israel is postponed,
and Paul the apostle to the Gentiles now takes over.

I would strongly suggest that the reader take time, before
going on, to read carefully, possibly several times, the chapters
relating the first foreign missionary journey by Paul and his
party. It will make it so much easier to follow Paul from place
to place and understand the missionary program as it was carried
on in the first century.

As we accompany Saul (Paul), Barnabas and John Mark
on their first missionary tour we shall have time to stop for only

a moment at each city. Then we shall see the general procedure common to the whole journey, rather than studying each stop in detail. Everywhere they went the story was the same. Let us join them as they begin this first interesting trip. We begin in the city of Antioch, not Jerusalem. They went forth from a local assembly, not from the apostolic mother in Jerusalem. They had no authority from the apostles, but went out independently. After leaving Antioch, a Gentile city far to the north of Jerusalem, they pass through Selucia where they took ship and sailed to the island of Cyprus, stopping at Salamis and Paphos. Here in Paphos we have the first detailed report. It is an interesting account:

> And when they had gone through the isle unto Paphos, they found a certain sorcerer, a false prophet, a Jew, whose name was Bar-jesus:
>
> Which was the deputy of the country, Sergius Paulus, a prudent man; who called for Barnabas and Saul, and desired to hear the word of God.
>
> But Elymas the sorcerer (for so is his name by interpretation) withstood them, seeking to turn away the deputy from the faith.
>
> Then Saul, (who also is called Paul,) filled with the Holy Ghost, set his eyes on him,
>
> And said, O full of all subtilty and all mischief, thou child of the devil, thou enemy of all righteousness, wilt thou not cease to pervert the right ways of the Lord?
>
> And now, behold, the hand of the Lord is upon thee, and thou shalt be blind, not seeing the sun for a season. And immediately there fell on him a mist and a darkness; and he went about seeking some to lead him by the hand.
>
> Then the deputy, when he saw what was done, believed, being astonished at the doctrine of the Lord (Acts 13:6-12).

We have quoted the entire account because of the tremendous dispensational picture of this present age. It occurs at the very outset of Paul's ministry to the Gentiles, right after the rejection of the Gospel message by Israel. Bar-jesus the sorcerer is a picture of national Israel in this age, dwelling out of their land among the Gentiles, holding important posts in world government. His name "Bar-jesus" means "son of Jehovah," but he is a false prophet. He is associated with the Gentile ruler, Sergius Paulus. All this is prophetic of the nation represented by this Bar-jesus. The ears of the Gentiles are open to the

Gospel, but this false prophet whom Paul addresses as "full of all subtilty and all mischief, thou child of the devil thou enemy of all righteousness," represents the nation of Israel in unbelief, as enemies of the Gospel and seeking to turn the Gentiles away from the truth. He represents the nation of the covenant set aside while the message goes to the Gentile world. In their rejection they are enemies of the Gospel. Paul says in Romans:

> As concerning the gospel, they are enemies for your sakes: but as touching the election, they are beloved for the fathers' sakes (Romans 11:28).

As a result of the opposition of this Jew, Bar-jesus, to the Gospel we have a picture of the blindness which is to characterize the nation during this dispensation. After describing this unbelieving enemy of the Gospel as full of subtilty and mischief, child of the devil, and enemy of righteousness, he pronounces a temporary blindness upon him. Notice carefully that this blindness upon Elymas was *temporary*. It was for a "season" only. I am sure you will see here the blindness Paul describes in Romans 11:25,

> For I would not, brethren, that ye should be ignorant of this mystery, lest ye should be wise in your own conceits; that *blindness in part is happened to Israel, until the fulness of the Gentiles be come in.*

This we believe is the teaching of the blindness of the first man who opposed Paul's ministry on his first missionary journey. It is placed at the very outset of the program to give us a picture of the temporary blindness and setting of the nation of Israel while the Gospel is going out to the Gentiles. And so the story ends with:

> Then the deputy, when he saw what was done, *believed* (Acts 13:12).

While Elymas is blinded, the Gentile deputy Sergius Paulus is saved. The setting aside of the nation results in the gathering in of the Church of Jesus Christ. After she is complete, God will take the scales from the eyes of His ancient covenant people and restore them fully, according to His unfailing promises. After this experience Paul and his party leave Paphos, take ship to Perga, in Asia Minor, and go by land immediately to Antioch (in Pisidia) and into the synagogue on the Sabbath day (Acts 13:14).

WHY GO TO THE JEWS?

Before taking up Paul's first recorded sermon on his missionary journey, we wish to point out one or two points of interest common to Paul's method and procedure in the various cities he visited. First, will you notice the name "Paul" is substituted for the name "Saul" (Acts 13:9). This is first done at Paphos at the very outset of his missionary career. Saul was his Hebrew name; Paul is the Greek equivalent. It is significant that as Paul turns to the nations, and his ministry is directed to the Gentiles, he drops his Jewish name and takes a Gentile name instead.

This raises another question. If the Gospel has gone to Israel and has been rejected, and now the message is to go to the Gentiles, then why does Paul still always go to the synagogue of the Jews upon his arrival? His first stop was Salamis and we are told,

> . . . they preached the word of God in the synagogues of the Jews . . . (Acts 13:5).

The same method is followed in verse 14; when they came to Antioch in Pisidia, they

> . . . went into the synagogue on the sabbath day . . .

The same procedure was followed in Iconium (Acts 14:1). Why did Paul go first on the Sabbath day to the synagogue? The answer is twofold:

1. Paul realized that while the nation of Israel as such had been rejected, the individuals in that nation had the same invitation to receive the Gospel as any Gentile. The fact that the nation had rejected the offer of the Kingdom did not mean that the individual Israelite was shut out from the Gospel of grace. The Church, the Body of Christ, consists of both Jew and Gentile. The message is the same to both, the requirements are the same, the privileges are the same, for

> . . . there is no difference between the Jew and the Greek [Gentile]: for the same Lord over all is rich unto all that call upon him.
>
> For *whosover* shall call upon the name of the Lord shall be saved (Romans 10:12, 13).

2. Moreover, Paul had a special love for his kinsmen according to the flesh. He grieved over their rejection of their

Messiah, and was burning with a desire to see as many individuals saved from this nation as possible. He says,

> Brethren, my heart's desire and prayer to God for Israel is, that they might be saved (Romans 10:1).

And listen to him again as he tells us with impassioned heart in Romans 9,

> I say the truth in Christ, I lie not, my conscience also bearing me witness in the Holy Ghost,
>
> That I have great heaviness and continual sorrow in my heart.
>
> For I could wish that myself were accursed from Christ for my brethren, my kinsman according to the flesh (Romans 9:1-3).

Here then is the reason Paul usually went to the synagogue first upon entering a new field. He wanted to offer the Gospel to his natural brethren first before any other.

3. There is another reason why Paul visited the synagogue first. Here he found a ready-made audience. It was the place where he could find a group of people already gathered to hear the Word. It was the logical place to go to introduce himself in a new area. This was the first place to start. When the synagogue was closed to him, he of course went elsewhere. This too was the reason Paul usually went in on the *Sabbath day*. Paul realized that the seventh-day Sabbath was not, nor ever had been for the Gentile, and that it has no place under grace, since the law was fulfilled in Christ. However, it was on the Sabbath day that the people attended the synagogue and this was an excellent time to reach these people. Paul fellowshiped with the Christians on the *first* day of the week to pray, to remember the Lord and to worship (Acts 20:7; I Corinthians 16:2). But he attended the synagogue on the Sabbath day only for the purpose of contacting and reaching the people. I trust you see why Paul, the apostle to the Gentiles, usually went first to the Jews in the synagogue on the Sabbath day. He became all things to all men, that he might by any means save some.

PAUL'S FIRST SERMON

This was the method Paul followed when he came to Antioch in Pisidia. He entered the synagogue and was invited to speak.

> Then Paul stood up, and beckoning with his hand said,
> Men of Israel, and ye that fear God, give audience (Acts
> 13:16).

Then follows Paul's sermon which we trust you will read carefully for yourself, as we can only point out the high spots of this first Pauline sermon (Acts 13:16-41). We would have you notice first to whom he addresses himself. It is to "men of Israel, and ye that fear God" (verse 16). He addresses first the men of Israel, and then includes Gentiles present as "ye that fear God." He then gives a detailed recital of Israel's past blessings and deliverances. He mentions first their deliverance from Egypt (verse 17). He traces God's faithfulness in the time of the judges (verse 20), and then God's leading under the kings, especially King David (verse 22). Then, having traced their history, he tells of the coming of the Messiah and how the nation had respected Him (verses 27 to 29). Paul relates how Christ was crucified, but "God raised Him from the dead" (verse 30). Having preached the Gospel — the death and resurrection of Christ — he now makes the application:

> Be it known unto you therefore, men and brethren, that
> through this man is preached unto you the forgiveness of sins:
> And by him all that *believed* are *justified* from all things,
> from which ye could not be justified by the law of Moses
> (Acts 13:38, 39).

This was a brand new message which had never been preached to them before. This was not the message of Peter at Pentecost. To be sure, Peter too had preached the Gospel of the death and resurrection of Jesus, and the offer of the Kingdom to the nation if they would receive Him as Messiah. It was addressed to the nation, and was definite:

> . . . Repent, and be baptized every one of you in the name
> of Jesus Christ for the remission of sins, and ye shall re-
> ceive the gift of the Holy Ghost (Acts 2:38).

This was not Paul's message now. He did not once mention repentance. He has nothing to say about baptism. He did not exhort them to do the best they could, or to live under the law as *they* had. Ah, no; that was the point of the new message — *the law of Moses could not save them,* and then he declares:

> And by him all that *believe are justified* from all things,
> from which ye could not be justified by the law of Moses
> (Acts 13:39).

The effect was electrifying! This was a new message. The Gentiles did not have to become Jews, did not have to be circumcised and keep the law of Moses, but could be *justified* by *just believing*. This is the simple message of grace. Great numbers believed and Paul was invited to come back the next Sabbath, which resulted in the first great opposition to Paul's message, and which caused Paul to throw all restraint to the winds, and tell them the result of their rejection.

> Then Paul and Barnabas waxed bold, and said, It was necessary that the word of God should first have been spoken to you [the Jews]: but seeing ye put it from you, and judge yourselves unworthy of everlasting life, lo, we turn to the Gentiles (Acts 13:46).

We take up the story from here in the next chapter, the Lord willing. Just a word of invitation. It is the new message of Paul —"all who believe are justified." Unsaved friend, the price is paid, the law has been satisfied. God has been reconciled, and you, no matter who or what you are, can be justified this moment if you will *believe on the Lord Jesus Christ* as your personal Saviour, for,

> . . . if thou shalt confess with thy mouth the Lord Jesus, and shalt believe in thine heart that God hath raised him from the dead, thou shalt be saved (Romans 10:9).

CHAPTER SEVENTEEN

Revival or Riot

The preaching of the Apostle Paul always had results. Wherever he preached, he either had a riot or a revival, and usually both. This was the case of Antioch:

> And when the Jews were gone out of the synagogue, the Gentiles besought that these words might be preached to them the next sabbath.

> And the next sabbath day came almost the whole city together to hear the word of God.

> But when the Jews saw the multitudes, they were filled with envy, and spake against those things which were spoken by Paul, contradicting and blaspheming.

> Then Paul and Barnabas waxed bold, and said, It was necessary that the word of God should first have been spoken to you: but seeing ye put it from you, and judge yourselves unworthy of everlasting life, lo, we turn to the Gentiles (Acts 13:42, 44-46).

This was the outcome of Paul's sermon in the synagogue at Antioch in Pisidia. They listened to Paul for a while, but when he offered the Gospel freely to the Gentiles it was too much for them, and the last straw came when Paul said, since you will not receive the message, "lo, we turn to the Gentiles."

> For so hath the Lord commanded us, saying, I have set thee to be a light of the Gentiles, that thou shouldest be for salvation unto the ends of the earth.

> And when the Gentiles heard this, they were glad, and glorified the word of the Lord: and as many as were ordained to eternal life believed.

> But the Jews stirred up the devout and honourable women, and the chief men of the city, and raised persecution against Paul and Barnabas, and expelled them out of their coasts.
>
> But they shook off the dust of their feet against them, and came unto Iconium (Acts 13:47, 48, 50, 51).

THE PATTERN FOR THIS AGE

This behavior in Antioch became the pattern for the opposition to the Gospel in every place where Paul goes to preach. Being expelled from Antioch, they travel on to Iconium some seventy-five miles to the east. The next chapter (Acts 14) relates the same history of persecution in Iconium which they had met in Antioch. It resulted in both a riot and a revival.

> And it came to pass in Iconium, that they went both together into the synagogue of the Jews, and so spake, that a great multitude both of the Jews and also of the Gentiles believed.
>
> But the unbelieving Jews stirred up the Gentiles, and made their minds evil affected against the brethren (Acts 14:1, 2).

It was again a revival and a riot. It was the same story over again. Opposition soon arose and,

> . . . when there was an assault made both of the Gentiles, and also of the Jews with their rulers, to use them despitefully, and to stone them,
>
> They were ware [aware] of it, and fled unto Lystra and Derbe, cities of Lycaonia, and unto the region that lieth round about (Acts 14:5, 6).

When Paul and Barnabas were driven out of one city, they did not lose heart and quit. They didn't go back home, but just moved on to the next place. They meant business and nothing could deter them. How we need men of that caliber today, who will not be discouraged by persecution and suffering, but who are strengthened by it instead and go on more determined than ever. Paul was not a quitter, ready to resign when the going became rough. How few there are who can meet problems head on, and face up to opposition and persecution without yielding to the temptation to quit.

ON TO DERBE AND LYSTRA

When the people in Iconium threatened to stone Paul and Barnabas they moved on to Derbe and Lystra, two cities only

a few miles from Iconium. In these cities things looked a bit more
promising for Paul and Barnabas, but it was not to be for long.
There was no synagogue in the city of Lystra because there
were not enough Jews there to organize one. Hence, there was
no immediate opposition from the leaders of the synagogue where
the trouble usually began. Where Paul preached, is not stated.
It may have been on a street corner or in the open market place.
Having no regular meeting place it was difficult to gather a
crowd, but the Lord had a way of giving them a hearing. There
was at least one man who listened to Paul, perhaps of necessity,
for he was a cripple unable to walk. As he sat by the way he
heard the words of Paul and evidently believed, for Paul saw
he had faith. Here was Paul's opportunity to get a crowd together. This man heard Paul, and Paul, perceiving he had faith
to be healed,

> Said with a *loud voice,* Stand upright on thy feet. And
> he leaped and walked (Acts 14:10).

At Paul's loud shout, many people were attracted and what
they saw amazed them, for this man who had been paralyzed
from birth, suddenly leaped up and began to walk around. The
miracle created a big stir, but before Paul could preach to them
something else happened. The people in Lycaonia were pagans,
worshiping many gods, and, beholding Paul and Barnabas as the
restorers of this lame man, they superstitiously supposed them
to be gods, and they

> . . . called Barnabas, Jupiter; and Paul, Mercurius . . .
> (Acts 14:12).

Believing them to be gods they began to prepare sacrifices
to them,

> Which when the apostles . . . heard of, they rent their
> clothes, . . . crying out,
> And saying, Sirs, why do ye these things? We also are men
> of like passions with you, and preach unto you that ye should
> turn from these vanities unto the living God.
> And with these sayings scarce restrained they the people,
> that they had not done sacrifice unto them (Acts 14:14, 15, 18).

It is to be noticed before we depart from Lystra with Paul,
that the apostles did not capitalize on the healing of this paralytic,
except to use it as an opening ledge to preach the Gospel to
these pagans. They did not start a great healing campaign and

turn the whole thing into a gigantic commercial venture. After they had quieted the multitude, trouble started from another quarter. As we said, there was no synagogue in Lystra, the city being almost entirely pagan, so Satan attacks the apostles from without importing the "rabble rousers" from other parts.

> And there came thither certain Jews from Antioch and Iconium, who persuaded the people, and, having stoned Paul, drew him out of the city, supposing he had been dead.
>
> Howbeit, as the disciples stood round about him, he rose up, and came into the city: and the next day he departed with Barnabas to Derbe (Acts 14:19, 20).

What a commentary on human nature! One moment ready to worship them; the next ready to kill them. This is as far as Paul and Barnabas go on this first missionary journey. They are now to retrace their steps back to Antioch, revisiting the cities in which they had preached. Before returning with them, we want to point out some practical lessons from the experience of Paul and Barnabas thus far.

1. The call to the full-time work of the Gospel is a divine call from God. Paul and Barnabas were not sent out by a church or denomination. They were ordained of God for the work (Acts 13:2).

2. There are some whom God has especially called, equipped and gifted for the special task of preaching. Not all have the same gifts. In the Church at Antioch were several prophets and teachers, but only Paul and Barnabas were sent out by the Holy Spirit.

3. Those who are thus called by God to discipleship, whether as missionaries, pastors, teachers, or other special areas of service, receive the call *for life*. There is no going back. One of the saddest things about modern-day missions is the alarming number of "fall outs." So many claim to have heard the special call for life service and go forth with enthusiasm and zeal, honestly and sincerely, only to fail when the test comes. When the going gets hard and persecution comes, they faint, and like John Mark who deserted Paul in Pamphylia; they come home defeated, disillusioned and even spoiled for service at home. We are to remember the words of our Lord:

> . . . No man, having put his hand to the plough, and looking back, is fit for the kingdom of God (Luke 9:62).

4. And this brings up a fourth observation. The Lord has no easy jobs, and no place for quitters. He has Himself promised,

> . . . In the world ye shall have tribulation: but be of good cheer; I have overcome the world (John 16:33).

If your service does not stir up the enemy, and your preaching does not produce opposition from Satan you may well question your faithfulness. There is a price attached to following Jesus in service. He said,

> . . . The servant is not greater than his lord. If they have persecuted me, they will also persecute you (John 15:20).

If you are not experiencing opposition to your testimony, you had better stop and take inventory.

5. The chief business of the missionary is to bring the Gospel to the people. If it is necessary to teach them to read and understand — well and good, but let it be only in order to get the Gospel to them. The primary business of the missionary is not to teach women to sew prettier dresses, or the men to raise better corn or build nicer houses. These things may become necessary on occasion, but all should be related to the Gospel. Teaching to sew, so they may be clothed instead of naked, will be the *result* of the preaching — not its chief aim. Healing the sick, building hospitals, holding clinics, are wonderful, if this missionary activity does not stop with the healing of the body. All these must be related to the preaching of the Gospel. Our commission is to preach salvation for eternity, not just relief from suffering for a time. All these other things are legitimate only as they serve as a wedge for the preaching of the Gospel of salvation.

6. A final lesson. We are to leave the results with the Lord. It is not our business to keep track of converts and to come back to the home church with a briefcase of statistics. It is a noteworthy fact that in the Bible *Gentile* converts are never counted. Only when God deals with Israel do we read of numbers. On Pentecost we are told 3000 were saved, but they were all Jews. In the fourth chapter of Acts the number rose to 5000, but they were all Jews. But not once in all the ministry to the Gentiles are numbers ever recorded. God only knows which ones to count and not to count. The numbering is for Israel, and is always on Kingdom ground. When the converts were all from Israel, their numbers are noted but no converts are numbered after the fourth chapter of Acts. Under the preaching of Paul we read

again and again that many believed, multitudes were saved, but *no numbers*. Only after the Church is raptured do numbers again appear, and we read of 144,000 of the twelve tribes of Israel saved during the Tribulation (Revelation 7 and 14).

BACK TO HOME BASE

These are some of the practical lessons we can learn from this first trip of the Apostle Paul. After Paul was stoned at Lystra, he and Barnabas revisited the cities in which they had preached.

> Confirming the souls of the disciples, and exhorting them to continue in the faith, and that we must through much tribulation enter into the kingdom of God (Acts 14:22).

And so on home to Antioch, ordaining elders on the way,

> And thence sailed to Antioch, from whence they had been recommended to the grace of God for the work which they fulfilled (Acts 14:26).

What a happy homecoming for the two pioneers, Paul and Barnabas! The church had a great welcoming party to listen to the interesting account of this *first missionary journey*. The chapter closes happily:

> And when they were come, and had gathered the church together, they rehearsed *all that God had done with them,* and how he had opened the door of faith unto the Gentiles.
> And there they abode long time with the disciples (Acts 14:27, 28).

They rehearsed what *God had done with them*. They did not come to tell what *they* had done, but *what God had done.* Evidently they gave no statistics or reported the number of converts. They left this up to the only One who knows. And so we would close with this personal question, "Are you numbered by God among those who have received eternal life? Or is your name on a church roll only? Or were you counted among those who signed a card at a meeting or raised your hand or came forward?" I do not object to belonging to a church, coming forward, signing a card, being baptized, any method at all, if it is an expression of your genuine, personal faith in Jesus Christ. But the important question is this: Is your name entered in the Lamb's book of life? If not, then do it now, and believe

> That if thou shalt confess with thy mouth the Lord Jesus, and shalt believe in thine heart that God hath raised him from the dead, thou shalt be saved (Romans 10:9).

CHAPTER EIGHTEEN

The First Ecumenical Council

A storm is brewing in the First Christian Church in the city of Jerusalem — a storm that is threatening to break at any moment. Disaster is prevented only by the action of the "First Ecumenical Council of Churches" in history, convened in the city of Jerusalem. The occasion for the calling of this ecumenical council was a sharp conflict between two different factions in the Early Church. Paul and Barnabas had gone on a missionary journey in Asia Minor. Their ministry had been largely to the Gentiles. They had just returned to Antioch and reported how the Gentiles had been saved by faith without becoming Jews, and without submitting to circumcision or placing themselves under the law of Moses. The Gentile Church at Antioch rejoiced in this good news, and the report spread to Jerusalem. Here it caused quite a stir among the legalistic members of the First Church in Jerusalem, who did not yet know the full truth of the grace of God. They still clung to the Law of Moses, and required circumcision and the customs of the Jews for all converts. Even the apostles themselves were not convinced of the genuineness of the pure gospel of grace which Paul preached. When the news of Paul's report that Gentiles were being saved by simply believing — plus nothing — reached Jerusalem, a group of legalistic teachers hurried down to Antioch and began to teach the believers there that Paul was wrong:

> And certain men which came down from Judaea taught the brethren, and said, Except ye [Gentiles] be circumcised after the manner of Moses, ye cannot be saved (Acts 15:1).

The fight was on, and the battle raged hot. Barnabas and Paul on the one hand were defending the grace of God, while these legalistic Judaizers from Jerusalem insisted upon circumcision and the keeping of the law. That there was a real church fight is quite evident from the record:

> When therefore Paul and Barnabas had no *small* (that means *big*) dissension and disputation with them, they determined that Paul and Barnabas, and certain other of them, should go up to Jerusalem unto the apostles and elders about this question (Acts 15:2).

THE FIRST ECUMENICAL COUNCIL

This was to be the first ecumenical council in church history, and Paul and Barnabas were delegates from Antioch. Before taking up the proceedings of this meeting we must fill in just a bit of material not mentioned here in Acts but revealed by Paul in his epistle to the Galatians (which, of course, was not yet written at the time of this meeting).

It seems that Peter had heard about the glowing report of Paul and Barnabas and personally had gone down to Antioch to get firsthand information. Paul and Barnabas were back from their first missionary trip and Peter pays them a visit. When Peter, an orthodox Jew, saw the evidence of the grace of God among these Gentile Christians, he cast off all his legal restraints, recognized the genuineness of Paul's message of grace, and entered fully and completely into fellowship with these Gentile believers. He ate with them, visited and fellowshiped with them as though there had never been any ancient or legal prejudices to separate them. He rejoiced with them in the liberty of grace.

Of course Peter already knew this, for when he was used to open the door to the house of Cornelius in Acts 10 the Lord had shown him, by means of the great sheet filled with all sorts of animals, that the middle wall between Jew and Gentile had broken down, and that God was no respecter of persons (Acts 10:34). Moreover, the apostles had agreed that Peter should stay in Jerusalem to minister to the Jews, while Paul was to go and bring the message to the Gentiles. Paul mentions this meeting in Galatians and tells us that when the apostles

. . . saw that the gospel of the uncircumcision was committed unto me, as the gospel of the circumcision was unto
Peter;

And when James, Cephas [Peter], and John, who seemed
to be pillars, perceived the grace that was given unto me, they
gave to me and Barnabas the right hands of fellowship; that
we should go unto the heathen, and they unto the circumcision (Galatians 2:7, 9).

After this agreement Peter goes to Antioch and enters fully
into fellowship with the Gentile Christians there, even eating
of their legally unclean foods. But then, when the legalistic
sabbatarian teachers from Jerusalem came to Antioch, Peter
withdrew himself from the group, because he was afraid of
the criticism of these legalistic, Judaistic law-teachers. This so
incensed Paul that he publicly rebukes and dresses Peter down
for his inconsistent conduct. But let us allow Paul to tell it in
his own words (Galatians 2:11-14).

But when Peter was come to Antioch, I withstood him
to the face, because he was to be blamed.

For before that certain [legalistic teachers] came from
James [in Jerusalem] he [Peter] did eat with the Gentiles:
but when they [the law teachers from Jerusalem] were come, he
withdrew and separated himself, fearing them which were of
the circumcision [the law].

But when I saw that they walked not uprightly according to the truth of the gospel, I said unto Peter before them
all, If thou, being a Jew, livest after the manner of Gentiles [as you've been doing since you came here] and not as
do the Jews, why compellest thou the Gentiles to live as do
the Jews?

This silenced Peter and we hear no more from him until they
meet for the general council in Jerusalem. But it only started
the battle in Antioch between Paul, the exponent of grace, and
the Jerusalem teachers of the law. The outcome was that to
prevent a split, they decided to go to Jerusalem and present
the case before the apostles. Paul and Barnabas and a few others
are appointed to go:

And being brought on their way by the church, they
passed through Phenice and Samaria, declaring the conversion
of the Gentiles: and they caused joy unto all the brethren
(Acts 15:3).

It is interesting to note what Paul and Barnabas did on their trip as delegates to the meeting of the "General synod" in Jerusalem. I don't know how they traveled, but they didn't spend their time lolling in ease, smoking cigars and playing cribbage in their luxurious stateroom. They were busy preaching all along the way. In this way they were "all fired up" when they arrived in Jerusalem, and they "declared all things that God had done with them." And now comes the critical moment when

> . . . there rose up certain of the sect of the Pharisees which believed, saying, That it was needful to circumcise them [the Gentiles], and to command them to keep the law of Moses.
>
> And the apostles and elders came together for to consider of this matter (Acts 15:5, 6).

First, the issue is stated. Here is the question: Are the Gentiles saved by grace through faith without circumcision or are they saved by being placed under the law? In other words, is it grace or is it law? Is it faith plus nothing, or is it faith plus the Ten Commandments? Plainly stated, it is: Are the Gentiles under the law? That was the issue; and although, as we shall see, it was settled nineteen hundred years ago, it is still a burning question today. Are we under law or under grace? Let us see the decision of this first ecumenical council. The question was not only: "Are we saved by grace through faith?" but it was "How are we kept *after* we are saved?" Oh yes, say the legalists, we are saved by grace, but then after that we are kept by works. We are saved by faith but then we must keep the law in order to remain saved. Paul had taught that we are saved and kept by grace. Let us be perfectly clear on the issue in question. The legalists say, "saved by grace and kept by keeping the law." That was the issue. The meeting is thrown open for discussion. The question is stated, and immediately it developed into a typical congregational meeting with arguing and disputing and wrangling.

> And when there had been much disputing, Peter rose up, and said unto them, Men and brethren, ye know how that a good while ago God made choice among us, that the Gentiles by my mouth should hear the word of the gospel, and believe.
>
> And God, which knoweth the hearts, bare them witness, giving them the Holy Ghost, even as he did unto us;

And put no difference between us and them, purifying
their hearts by faith.

Now therefore why tempt ye God, to put a yoke upon
the neck of the disciples [Gentile believers], which neither
our fathers nor we were able to bear?

But we believe that through the grace of the Lord Jesus
Christ we shall be saved, even as they (Acts 15:7-11).

Well spoken, Peter — very well spoken! He reminds them
first how it was he himself who had used the keys of the Kingdom to open up the Gospel to the Gentiles in the house of
Cornelius (Acts 10). Then he reminds these legalists that they
are requiring something of the Gentiles which neither they nor
their fathers were able to do; viz., keep the law perfectly. They
needed grace, for the law only condemned them. Peter's testimony had quite an effect upon the assembly and they quietly
listened to what Paul and Barnabas had to say:

Then all the multitude kept silence, and gave audience to
Barnabas and Paul, declaring what miracles and wonders
God had wrought among the Gentiles by them (Acts 15:12).

The Big Question

The testimony of Peter, Paul and Barnabas was indeed convincing and conclusive. They could not say anything against it,
but it immediately raised another question. If the Gospel is now
open to the Gentiles, and the Church is being formed of both
Jews and Gentiles, then what about all the hundreds and hundreds of prophecies concerning the Messianic Kingdom? What
about Christ sitting upon the throne of David in Jerusalem?
Then what about the restoration of the nation of Israel and the
defeat of their oppressors and conquerors? Is God all through
with national Israel, and has the Church taken Israel's place?
Is the Church now spiritual Israel? These were questions which
had to be answered. These were questions uppermost in the
minds of the apostles before Jesus left them. They believed
in the literal setting up of the Messianic Kingdom upon earth,
and they asked Christ repeatedly about the time. Even at the
Mount of the Ascension they were still looking for the Kingdom.
They knew nothing about the Church of this age. That was
a mystery to be revealed only after Pentecost. And so they had
asked the Lord their last question before He went away:

> . . . Lord, wilt thou at this time restore again the king-
> dom to Israel? (Acts 1:6).

The Lord did not tell them to forget about the Kingdom and
the restoration of Israel, but told them it was not for them to
know the time. While they were waiting, they were to carry out
His commission to be "witnesses in Jerusalem, Judaea, Samaria
and all the world." This new program was hard to accept. And
so when Paul and Barnabas, together with Peter, brought forth
indisputable evidence that the Church and not the Kingdom was
being built, and that the Gentiles were included, it was hard
to accept; but being forced to accept it, they were left with an
all-important question. If God is now building the Church,
then what about all the promises of the kingdom of David on
earth? ¿Must all those prophecies be spiritualized and applied to
the Church instead? This question must be settled. If the
Church is the Kingdom, then the requirements of the Kingdom
must be met, and the Gentiles must be circumcised and brought
under the law of the Kingdom. After a long significant silence,
God gives the answer to this question. James, who seems to be
the chairman of the meeting, speaks and clears up the entire
matter. His answer is in Acts 15:13-18. We strongly urge that
you read carefully these six verses in Acts 15 before proceeding
to the next chapter. In these verses the Holy Spirit once and for
all settles the question of the reason for this Church Age intervening between the First and Second Coming of Christ, and
establishes the certainty of the setting up of the Messianic Kingdom at the return of the Messiah.

This answer of James we take up in our next chapter.

CHAPTER NINETEEN

Are the Gentiles Under Law?

The first great ecumenical council of Christian Churches was held in the city of Jerusalem in about A.D. 52, almost twenty years after Jesus went back to Heaven. The host church was the "First Christian Church" in Jerusalem, and its pastor, James, the brother of our Lord, was the chairman of the meeting. The occasion for this first meeting of the "general synod" was a vexing controversy over the position of Gentile converts in this church. Paul had preached salvation by grace through faith *plus nothing*. The Judaizing believers in Jerusalem claimed that in order for Gentiles to be saved they must become Jews, submit to circumcision and keep the laws of Moses. They said,

> . . . Except ye be circumcised after the manner of Moses, ye cannot be saved (Acts 15:1).

And in verse 5 we read that these legalists said:

> . . . That it was needful to circumcise them and to command them to keep the law of Moses (Acts 15:5).

The controversy waxed hotter and hotter until they reached an impasse, and it was decided to consult the apostles and elders in Jerusalem for an answer.

THE GREAT MEETING

At this ecumenical meeting Peter agrees with Paul, and Paul rehearses how God had moved among the Gentiles. The evidence was so overwhelming that they had no answer. They must agree that the Gentiles as well as Jews are saved by grace without the works of the law, and that Christ was now building a new thing, the Body of Christ, the Church, from among all peoples, tongues and tribes and nations. But it raised one *big* question. If God is now building a Church of all peoples, then what about the thousands of prophecies concerning the restoration of the kingdom of Israel, the deliverance of the nation, their return to the Promised Land, and Messiah sitting on David's throne, while Jesus the Messiah reigned *upon* this earth over all the nations? Have we misunderstood the promises of a literal Kingdom on earth, and is the Church now spiritual Israel? This was the question, and now we come to the answer:

> And after they had held their peace, James answered, saying, Men and brethren, hearken unto me:
>
> Simeon [Peter] hath declared how God at the first did visit the Gentiles, to take out of them a people for his name (Acts 15:13, 14).

Yes, declares James, I agree with Peter and Paul that God is dealing today with the Gentiles. He is visiting the nations and saving individuals regardless of nationality or relationship. All this is true. God *is* visiting the Gentiles to take out of them a people for His Name. He *is* building a Church composed of both Jew and Gentile during this dispensation. But, says James, this does not set aside the Kingdom promises, or nullify the prophecies concerning the promised age of blessing and peace when Israel is restored under the personal presence of Messiah. The fact that God is now taking out from among the Gentiles a Church is not in conflict with the prophetic promises of the Kingdom. To the contrary, this is all according to God's foreknown plan. And so James continues:

> And to this agree the words of the prophets; as it is written,
>
> After this I will return, and will build again the tabernacle of David, which is fallen down; and I will build again the ruins thereof, and I will set it up:
>
> That the residue of men might seek after the Lord, and all the Gentiles, upon whom my name is called, said the Lord, who doeth all these things.
>
> Known unto God are all his works from the beginning of the world (creation) (Acts 15:15-18).

This is one of the most important passages in the New Testament. Dispensationally it gives God's plan and purpose for this Church Age, and the beginning of the Kingdom Age. Peter says

first God is taking out from among the Gentiles a people for His
Name. This is the Church, born at Pentecost, and consisting of
Jew and Gentile without difference. The word "church" in the
original is *ecclesia* or a *called out* assembly. The Gospel in this
age will not save the masses, but instead "calls out" one here
and a few there. Nowhere in the Bible does it promise the conversion of the world in this age. Nowhere in history are whole
cities converted, but some here and some there. When this
number, ordained to be saved, is complete, the Church will be
caught away. Notice James says:

> After this I will return, and will build again the taber-
> nacle of David, which is fallen down . . . (Acts 15:16).

Notice the words *after this* I will return to set up the Kingdom.
And we ask, *after what?* And the answer is *after* God has taken
out from among the Gentiles a people for His Name. This is the
program of God. When Jesus came the first time to offer the
Kingdom to Israel it was rejected, the nation was set aside, and
God revealed a new thing — the Church, the Body of Christ
which would fill the interim between our Lord's rejection and
His coming to set up the Throne of David. This is what He is
doing today, "calling out" the Church, the Bride of the King,
and *then after* that He will return and fulfill all the Kingdom
promises. So to the question, Has the Lord forgotten Israel? Is
the Church the Kingdom? — to this James says *no!* When the last
member is added to the Body of Christ, the Lord will return,
restore Israel, and bring in the glorious millennial age of peace.
This, too, the Apostle Paul asserts when he answers the question in Romans 11:1,

> I say then, Hath God cast away his people (Israel)? . . .

The final answer is found in verses 25-27:

> For I would not, brethren, that ye should be ignorant
> of this mystery, lest ye should be wise in your own conceits;
> that blindness in part is happened to Israel, *until* the fulness
> of the Gentiles be come in.
>
> And so all Israel shall be saved: as it is written, There
> shall come out of Sion the Deliverer, and shall turn away un-
> godliness from Jacob:
>
> For this is my covenant unto them, when I shall take
> away their sins.

This is in perfect harmony with the statement of James in Acts 15:16, *After this* I will return. And then notice the next verse:

> That the residue of men might seek after the Lord, and all the Gentiles, upon whom my name is called, saith the Lord, who doeth all these things (Acts 15:17).

First then the Church must be called out. Then Christ will return and Israel will be converted and settled in her land, and then the Gospel will be preached by redeemed Israel to all the world till every tongue shall confess and every knee bow to the King of Kings. This is God's long-range program. The Bible does not promise the conversion of the world in this age. It does not even promise a majority, but instead only a remnant, a *called out* group will be saved. The great world-wide revival will come only after Israel's conversion, and all the world will be won for Christ,

> When He shall have dominion
> Over land and sea;
> And earth's remotest regions
> Shall His empire be.

This postponement of the Kingdom and the calling out of the Church in this age was a mystery, unknown until after Pentecost. At the first coming of Christ, Israel expected that as Messiah He would deliver them immediately from the yoke of Gentile bondage and restore the Kingdom. The introduction of the Church was therefore a great surprise and a mystery of which Paul says,

> . . . that by revelation he [God] made known unto me the mystery: (as I wrote afore in few words,
>
> Whereby, when ye read, ye may understand my knowledge in the *mystery* of Christ)
>
> Which in other ages was not made known unto the sons of men, as it is now revealed unto his holy apostles and prophets by the Spirit (Ephesians 3:3-5).

Now what was this mystery not revealed heretofore?

> *That the Gentiles* should be fellowheirs, and of the same body, and partakers of his promise in Christ by the gospel (Ephesians 3:6).

This mystery was not unknown to God but was part of His great plan for the ages, and so James concludes:

> Known unto God are all his works from the beginning of the world (Acts 15:18).

Now we go back to the question which brought the members of the ecumenical council to Jerusalem. You remember the question: Must Gentiles, in order to be saved, be circumcised and must they keep the law of Moses? (Acts 15:5). Here is the answer of James which was unanimously endorsed by the apostles and elders:

> Wherefore my sentence is, that we trouble not them, which from among the Gentiles are turned to God:

> But that we write unto them, that they abstain from pollutions of idols, and from fornication, and from things strangled, and from blood (Acts 15:19, 20).

Idolatry and fornication were the two chief sins of the Gentiles. They were warned against these, and also eating of blood which antedated the law by almost nine hundred years (Genesis 9:4). A letter from the council at Jerusalem was drafted and sent by the hands of Paul, Barnabas and two others to the Gentile church at Antioch. The letter was brief and to the point:

> . . . The apostles and elders and brethren send greeting unto the brethren which are of the Gentiles in Antioch and Syria and Cilicia:

> Forasmuch as we have heard, that certain which went out from us have troubled you with words, subverting your souls, saying, Ye must be circumcised, and keep the law: *to whom we gave no such commandment* (Acts 15:23, 24).

Notice the answer. The apostles said that those who taught that the Gentiles were under the law, had no authority to teach this at all. They declare, *we gave no such commandment.* Although this question of the law was settled here nineteen hundred years ago, the legalists of today are just as determined to put us back under law as were the Pharisees of that day. Heed carefully the words of the council:

> For it seemed good to the Holy Ghost, and to us, to lay upon you no greater burden than these necessary things;

> That ye abstain from meats offered to idols, and from

> blood, and from things strangled, and from fornication: from which if ye keep yourselves, ye shall do well. Fare ye well (Acts 15:28, 29).

The letter was delivered to the believers in Antioch, who when they had read the epistle,

> . . . rejoice for the consolation.
>
> And Judas and Silas, being prophets also themselves, exhorted the brethren with many words, and confirmed them.
>
> And after they had tarried there a space, they were let go in peace from the brethren unto the apostles.
>
> Notwithstanding it pleased Silas to abide there still.
>
> Paul also and Barnabas continued in Antioch, teaching and preaching the word of the Lord, with many others also (Acts 15:31-35).

What a happy ending to a stormy beginning! The 15th chapter of Acts opens with contention and quarreling among the brethren over the question of law and grace, but, thank God, grace prevailed. And so the chapter with such a stormy beginning ended up peacefully. Chapter 15 of Acts should logically end at verse 35, and the 16th chapter should begin with verse 36, which introduces us to Paul's second missionary journey. This second journey had a very sad beginning. The two buddies, Paul and Barnabas, had a falling out and broke up. It seems impossible that this could happen. They had suffered so much together, and now they separate as the result of a quarrel. After the council session in Jerusalem, Paul suggested to Barnabas that they go and visit all the churches they had established on their first journey. But Barnabas determined to take along John Mark. This John Mark had started on the first missionary journey with them, but had "quit" when the going became rough and had gone back home. Now Barnabas wanted to take him along again, but Paul said "nothing doing."

> But Paul thought not good to take him with them, who departed from [deserted] them from Pamphylia . . . (Acts 15:38).

A real spat resulted, tempers rose,

> And the contention was so sharp between them, that they departed asunder one from the other: and so Barnabas took Mark, and sailed unto Cyprus;

And Paul chose Silas, and departed, . . .
And he went through Syria and Cilicia, confirming the
churches (Acts 15:39-41).

How tragic! How sad! Here are Paul and Barnabas, who had
labored together on their first trip, had suffered together and
stuck together through thick and thin, and now have come to
a misunderstanding and a split over John Mark who had deserted them once before. And the quarrel ended in the breakup
of the team God had so mightily used before. Barnabas takes
Mark, sails to Cyprus and drops into oblivion. We have no
further word about their ministry in Cyprus. How sad these
painful experiences! I am sure that Paul had looked forward
to this second journey of fellowship with Barnabas and remembered the blessed days they had spent together; and now over
an unjustifiable loyalty to a man who had proven unreliable,
Barnabas forsakes one of the best friends he ever had. Surely we
are reminded that the saintliest of men still need to be on guard
against the enemy of our souls. Poor Barnabas! He was the loser
for allowing his loyalty to his friend Mark to cause a break with
God's man Paul, but how it must have grieved the heart of Paul
as well. God help us to heed the lesson. There is nothing quite
so sad as to see two servants of God, after laboring together,
facing trials and suffering, come to a misunderstanding over
a personality or minor difference of opinion and break up and
go their separate ways. Barnabas was willing to desert his God-
given call to the ministry because of a quarrel over an unde-
pendable friend. Oh, that we might learn the lesson and profit
by it.

CHAPTER TWENTY
Paul's First Mistake

The great ecumenical council of the Church of Jesus Christ was held in the city of Jerusalem in about A.D. 52, only twenty years after its beginning at Pentecost. The question to be settled was, Are the Gentiles under the Law of Moses, and must they be circumcised? The verdict was a positive no! Peter, in giving his experience says that God,

> . . . put no difference between us [Jews] and them [Gentiles], purifying their hearts by faith.
> Now therefore why tempt ye God, to put a yoke upon the neck of the disciples, which neither our fathers nor we were able to bear?
> But we believe that through the grace of the Lord Jesus Christ we shall be saved, even as they (Acts 15:9-11).

Peter calls the law a yoke which neither they nor their fathers were able to bear. No one was ever saved by keeping the law, then or now. The law was given to show the *need* of salvation, but it could not *provide* salvation. To this the council agreed, and it was decided that salvation for the Gentiles did not require circumcision and was not by keeping the law, but was given by grace.

THE SECOND MISSIONARY JOURNEY

Soon after this matter was settled Paul proposes a second missionary tour with Barnabas, his partner on the first trip. But a dispute arose between Paul and Barnabas over John Mark, the deserter who had left them in the lurch on the first trip. Barnabas stuck by his friend. He and Paul parted and Paul took Silas and started on his second tour. From here (Acts 16 to 28)

we have an account of Paul's second and third missionary
journeys, and his final trip as a prisoner to Rome. The book
closes with Paul in jail (Acts 28:31). Time will not permit us
to go into a detailed discussion of these last thirteen chapters of
Acts. We shall follow hurriedly along with Paul, stopping here
and there to give particular attention to certain outstanding
incidents in the last ten years of Paul's life. After he and Barnabas
parted, Paul visited Syria and Cilicia by land north of Antioch,
and then revisited Derbe and Lystra where he had healed the
lame man. Here a very important event took place in the life
of Paul:

> Then came he [Paul] to Derbe and Lystra: and, behold,
> a certain disciple was there, named Timotheus, the son of
> a certain woman, which was a Jewess, and believed; but his
> father was a Greek:
>
> Which was well reported of by the brethren that were at
> Lystra and Iconium (Acts 16:1, 2).

Timothy's mother was Eunice and his grandmother Lois, both
godly women who had trained Timothy well.

> Him would Paul have to go forth with him; and took and
> circumcised him because of the Jews which were in those
> quarters: for they knew all that his father was a Greek
> (Acts 16:3).

Can this be true? Did Paul actually circumcise Timothy because he was afraid of the criticism of the Jews? Can it be possible that this is the same Paul who had everywhere preached
salvation by grace *plus nothing?* Unbelievable, but alas, all
too true. Think of it! Paul had just come from the council at
Jerusalem where it was decided once for all that the believers
did not have to be circumcised. And here he compromises that
very position. Can this be the same Paul who later wrote in
Galatians 2 that when he went to Jerusalem,

> But neither Titus, who was with me, being a Greek,
> was compelled to be circumcised:
>
> And that because of [in spite of] false brethren unawares
> brought in, who came in privily to spy out our liberty which
> we have in Christ Jesus, that they might bring us into bondage:
>
> To whom we gave place by subjection, no, not for an hour;
> that the truth of the gospel might continue with you (Gala-
> tians 2:3-5).

Here was a parallel case. Titus, a Greek, was taken by Paul
to Jerusalem. There certain legalists were secretly spying on Paul
to see whether he would circumcise Titus, but Paul would not
budge an inch; he stood his ground. Yet here in the case of
Timothy, Paul compromises the grace of God and circumcises
Timothy "because of the Jews." Can this be the same Paul who
wrote later,

> For in Jesus Christ neither circumcision availeth any thing,
> nor uncircumcision; but faith which worketh by love (Gala-
> tians 5:6).

ALL THINGS TO ALL MEN

There are those who defend Paul's action by saying he merely
accommodated himself in order to win his critics by "becoming
all things to all men." But no one has a right to violate the truth,
to compromise the Gospel, to water down the message and cut
corners in order not to offend those we are trying to win. We
can never win men and women by conceding to their error or
cooperating in their false program. No, we simply cannot excuse
Paul. His motive may have been of the best, and prompted by his
desire to win his brethren according to the flesh, his purpose
may have been pure, but his conduct was wrong. This was the
first step in Paul's compromising backsliding which as we shall
see ended him finally in a prison in Rome. We realize this
shocks some people who consider Paul as virtually infallible.
While we believe when he wrote the epistles he wrote infallibly
under the guidance of the Holy Spirit, still Paul was as human
as we are. He says to the people of Lycaonia, "we also are men
of like passions as you." There is such a tendency to "canonize"
the heroes of the Bible, as though they could not make mistakes.
To find fault with Moses is to some folks blasphemy. To criticize
father Abraham is to some folks a mortal sin. To point out the
failings of Jacob is to evidence racial discrimination. Yet the
evidence of the divine nature of the Bible is that it does not
cover up the faults of the heroes or magnify the vices of the
villains. It treats all with equal fairness, for God is no respecter
of persons. The Bible tells us of Noah who walked with God,
but it also records his drunken stupor. It records Moses as the
meekest man, but also tells of his rebellion and temper. It calls
David the man after God's own heart, but does not hesitate to
give the record of his unspeakable sin. And so we might go on.

Paul was no exception. The purpose of the Bible is *not* to exalt
the perfections and goodness of men, not even the godliest of
saints, but to exalt the *grace* of God, and the more unworthy
the object of His love, the greater the grace. Paul has been called
the "apostle of grace," and we shall see how God used him as
an example of abounding grace. We shall trace the downward
path of Paul's tragic mistake in our coming messages.

BARNABAS AND TIMOTHY

We leave for the moment this unpleasant incident in Paul's life,
and point out a more pleasant and consoling one. In Lystra Paul
found Timothy who was to be closely associated with him until
the very end. The timing of the Lord was perfect. No better
time could have been chosen for Paul to find his beloved
Timothy. Paul's heart must have been very heavy. Just a few
days before he had experienced one of the most bitter disap-
pointments in his life. A faithful, beloved companion had forsaken him. Barnabas had stuck by Paul throughout his entire
first missionary journey in tribulation, persecution, stonings and
threatenings. And then in a squabble over a "friend" who had
proven untrue, Barnabas forsakes Paul who had been so close
to him and "sticks by" his friend John Mark even though it meant
parting with Paul. How heavy his heart must have been. Few
things are harder to bear than to be forsaken by those whom
you have labored with, prayed with, suffered with and rejoiced
with, and then over some personal grievance they leave us. It
is hard to understand why some for whom we have done the
most, will turn against us when we need them the most. I am
sure Paul came to Lystra with a broken heart. But the Lord was
waiting with balm for his broken heart when he came to Lystra,
for there he found

TIMOTHY

He lost a Barnabas, but God gave him a Timothy. And what
a joy he was to be in the days ahead. How he became endeared
to Paul. With what faithfulness young Timothy served Paul to
the very end. He was probably led to Christ by Paul, for he
calls him "my own son in the faith" (I Timothy 1:2) and "my
dearly beloved son" (II Timothy 1:2). How gracious of the Lord
to send Timothy into Paul's life at this very time. He proved
more loyal than Barnabas, for Timothy never wavered or for-

sook Paul. When God allows precious things to be taken out of our lives we may rest assured it is for a purpose, and if we wait for the answer, He has something better in store for us. And how happy we are that the Bible also relates a reconciliation between Paul and Barnabas and Mark. Just before Paul's death, while in the prison at Rome, he wrote to the Colossians:

> Aristarchus my fellowprisoner saluteth you, and *Marcus,* sister's son to Barnabas, (touching whom ye received commandments: if he come unto you, receive him;) (Colossians 4:10).

Paul had forgiven John Mark who caused the painful break in fellowship between himself and his closest associate, Barnabas. He is afraid the Colossians would remember the ill treatment Paul had suffered because of Mark, and might not give him a welcome, so he writes, "if he come unto you, receive him."

The balance of Acts 16 records the well-known account of Paul's call to Europe. He had planned to go east into Asia, but the Lord prevented him and pointed him to the west instead. He saw a man of Macedonia in a vision beckoning him and saying,

> . . . Come over to Macedonia, and help us (Acts 16:9).

Paul was not disobedient to the heavenly vision but crossed over into Macedonia and came to Philippi, evidently looking for the man he had seen in the vision, and instead he found a *woman.* He preached at a women's prayer meeting at the riverside (there was no synagogue in Philippi), and Lydia, a native of Thyatira, believed, was saved and was baptized. Lydia was from Asia, and now Paul could see the reason for the Lord preventing him from going into Asia. The Lord has an indirect way of getting the Gospel there by the conversion of a native of Asia while in a prayer meeting in Europe. Undoubtedly this traveling saleswoman, Lydia, carried the message to her home country, saving Paul the trip. The Lord moves in a mysterious way His wonders to perform.

Next we have the imprisonment of Paul and Silas and their miraculous deliverance, followed by the conversion of the Philippian jailor. We do not dwell at length on this incident, so familiar to all, except to point out the message Paul preached to these Gentiles. It was the same Gospel of the death and resurrection of Christ which Peter preached at Pentecost, but an entirely different application. Peter's admonition to Israel was:

> . . . Repent, and be baptized every one of you in the name of Jesus Christ for the remission of sins . . . (Acts 2:38).

This was not Paul's message. It was instead:

> . . . Believe on the Lord Jesus Christ, and thou shalt be saved, and thy house (Acts 16:31).

It is interesting to note that Luke, the author of Acts, was with Paul in Philippi. Although he is not mentioned by name, the pronoun "they" changes to "we" in verse 10. Up until Paul reached Troas, ready to go to Philippi, Luke says:

> And *they* [Paul and his company] . . . came down to Troas (Acts 16:8).

Here in Troas Paul receives the Macedonian call (verse 9) and then in verse 10 we read:

> And . . . immediately *we* endeavoured to go into Macedonia (Acts 16:10).

Evidently Dr. Luke joins Paul at this point. And from here Luke becomes Paul's constant companion and personal physician, remaining with him to the end. We know that Paul had some chronic physical infirmity which probably needed frequent medical attention. Paul refers to this as a "thorn in the flesh" which he called a "messenger of Satan to buffet" him (II Corinthians 12:7). This ailment, whatever it was, became a source of great concern to Paul. Some think Paul was a hunchback (based on II Corinthians 10:10). Others thought he suffered from ophthalmia, as a result of the blinding light on the Damascus road. This idea is based on Galatians 4:13, Galatians 4:15 and Galatians 6:11. Others think it was malaria, but why go on, for they are all only guesses. Evidently it was an incurable disease and yet the Lord was not pleased to heal him although he prayed earnestly. He tells us:

> For this thing I besought the Lord thrice, that it might depart from me (II Corinthians 12:8).

But the Lord said *no!* and Paul accepted God's answer. While he was not healed, the Lord provided him with a good doctor, instead, to take care of him. Dr. Luke joins the party at Troas and stays with him. How wonderful to be able to say, "Thy will be done" and wait for the Lord to give grace and provide relief in another way. Are you afflicted, sick and weak? Do you desire relief and healing? There is nothing wrong with this, but you must be willing to abide by God's decision. If it pleases Him *not* to grant your request, you can either be a miserable, rebellious and unhappy person, or you can be a happy sufferer saying, "Not my will, but Thine be done." If it is for His glory and my good that my desires are not granted, then believe that the Father knows best. Thank Him for a good physician, and above all for the Great Physician who will not suffer you to be tested above that which you are able to bear. There is no greater peace than that which leaves the decision with the Lord.

CHAPTER TWENTY-ONE

Mistaken Zeal

What do people in jail sing about? Not many prisoners feel like singing, but if they do, what can they sing about? It certainly must have sounded strange when the prisoners in a Philippian jail heard two men singing psalms and hymns. Yet that is what Paul and Silas did while their hands and feet were in stocks. It was powerful singing too. All this is recorded in the sixteenth chapter of Acts, resulting in the conversion of the Philippian jailor and his family. After being released from prison they went to the city of Thessalonica and remained there about two weeks and were once more driven out to save their lives. They went to Berea and here it was again the same story. They went into the synagogue, but here too they were soon driven out. It was the same story everywhere. Paul first went (whenever possible) to the synagogue where he could find a ready-made audience, but in every case was soon driven out. We pass over this journey rapidly because it is the same experience everywhere. Driven out of Berea, they journeyed to Athens where he preached only one sermon, a masterpiece of oratory but without any great results. No church was established. After his great oration on Mars Hill they ridiculed Paul and he left in deep disappointment. Only a few people were interested and so Paul departs for Corinth, another great European city.

PAUL'S MINISTRY IN CORINTH

We have passed over Paul's experience in Thessalonica, Berea and Athens rather rapidly for the story was the same in every place. But when he comes to Corinth there is a different experience. Here he meets two precious friends, Aquila and Priscilla.

Paul as usual goes into the synagogue and preaches the Gospel. Here he is joined by Silas and Timothy whom he had left behind in Macedonia. Once again he meets with the same opposition, and we read:

> And when they opposed themselves, and blasphemed, he [Paul] shook his raiment, and said unto them, Your blood be upon your own heads; I am clean: from henceforth I will go unto the Gentiles.
> And he departed thence, and entered into a certain man's house, named Justus, one that worshipped God, whose house joined hard to the synagogue (Acts 18:6, 7).

This is a pivotal passage. This is the first time Paul leaves the synagogue voluntarily. Before this he had always been forced out but now he walks out and enters into a house adjoining the synagogue. The witness to Israel is about to end. The Church began at Pentecost with not a single Gentile, but as we move on in our journey through Acts, the Jewish element gradually declines and becomes more largely Gentile in character. As the transition from Judaism to Christianity and from law to grace progresses, special miracles, signs and wonders gradually diminish (these were Kingdom signs committed to the apostles during the apostolic age) until they disappear entirely. After the completion of the New Testament the need for verifications of the Gospel by signs, wonders and miracles are no more needed.

This experience of Paul in leaving the synagogue and his beloved brethren after the flesh caused Paul to become greatly discouraged. He was ready to leave, but the Lord came to the rescue.

> Then spake the Lord to Paul in the night by a vision, Be not afraid, but speak, and hold not thy peace:
> For I am with thee, and no man shall set on thee to hurt thee: for I have much people in this city.
> And he continued there a year and six months, teaching the word of God among them (Acts 18:9-11).

How blessed God's provision! Paul was greatly discouraged and depressed. Read the first epistle to the Corinthians for a glimpse into Paul's heart. But the Lord came to encourage him. He stayed on for a year and a half, and a great congregation was established in Corinth. After his unusually long stay in Corinth, Paul moves on to Ephesus. (I do trust you are follow-

ing us with Paul on this trip by reading carefully the account
in Acts 18 and 19.)

Before we depart with Paul from Corinth, we must mention a
tragic mistake of Paul before he left Corinth.

> And Paul after this tarried there [in Corinth] yet a good
> while, . . . and sailed thence into Syria, . . . ; having shorn
> his head in Cenchrea: for he had a vow (Acts 18:18).

We come here to the second step in the tragic mistake of
Paul in compromising the Gospel which led to his imprisonment.
The first step you will remember was the circumcising of Timothy in Lystra at the beginning of this second missionary journey.
Now Paul takes a legal vow. Paul, the great exponent of grace,
places self under a legal obligation, taking a vow, and shaving
his head to indicate he had thus committed himself! This vow
was to end disastrously. It is impossible to defend Paul in this
inconsistent action. Having taken this vow, Paul goes to Ephesus
but he now becomes restless and uneasy. His vow and his decision to go to Jerusalem seems to overshadow even his commission to preach the Gospel. At Ephesus he was well received in
the synagogue and they invited Paul to stay longer (something
unheard of before). But Paul refused:

> When they desired him to tarry longer time with them,
> But bade them farewell, saying, I must by all means keep
> this feast that cometh in Jerusalem: but I will return again
> unto you, if God will. And he sailed from Ephesus (Acts
> 18:20, 21).

He leaves Ephesus in haste, and the reason he gives is his
determination to reach Jerusalem to keep the feast of Pentecost.
This determination became an obsession with him, and he becomes more and more hurried until he again reaches Ephesus.
In this city he is forcibly reminded that he had no business going
to Jerusalem or to go back under the law. In Ephesus he met
twelve men who were still under the law from which Paul had
been delivered. When Paul meets them he notices something
wrong about their testimony:

> He said unto them, Have ye received the Holy Ghost
> since [when] ye believed? And they said unto him, We have
> not so much as heard whether there be any Holy Ghost.
> And he said unto them, Unto what then were ye bap-
> tized? And they said, Unto John's baptism.

> Then said Paul, John verily baptized with the baptism of
> repentance, saying unto the people, that they should believe
> on him which should come after him, that is, on Jesus Christ.
> When they heard this, they were baptized in the name of
> the Lord Jesus (Acts 19:2-5).

Their baptism was followed by the gift of tongues and prophecy. This is the very last time tongues are mentioned in the book of Acts. These twelve men had only heard the gospel of the Kingdom. They knew about Jesus as Messiah, and were baptized with John's baptism. Paul asks, "Have ye received the Holy Ghost *when* ye believed?" the word "since" should be *when*. A quick reference to your concordance or Greek lexicon will show this. The mistranslation of the word "since" instead of *when* has given rise to the teaching of a baptism of the Holy Spirit after one is saved, whereas every believer is baptized when he is saved, for

> . . . if any man have not the Spirit of Christ, he is none
> of his (Romans 8:9).

This last mention of the gift of tongues in Acts is the final evidence that the apostolic age is drawing to a close. As the books of the New Testament began to be written, the need for confirming evidences disappears. After this experience Paul continues preaching in the synagogue until he once again leaves to hold his meetings in a neutral place, and

> . . . he departed from them, and separated the disciples,
> disputing daily in the school of one Tyrannus (Acts 19:9).

The rest of the experiences of Paul in Ephesus we must pass over but we recommend that you read this chapter (Acts 19) before we take up the next chapter.

We remind you again that wherever Paul went he either had a revival or a riot. Sometimes it was both, and too often the revival was the cause of the riot. True to this pattern, it was the experience of Paul in the city of Ephesus on his second missionary journey. He had begun preaching in the synagogue (Acts 19:8) but soon found conditions there so unbearable that he left the established place of worship, and took a group of disciples with him to a neutral place in a school auditorium. Today Paul would be called a "church splitter," a non conformist, and a fundamentalist.

After Paul had led his "secession" he spent about two years of fruitful ministry in the city of Ephesus. The epistle to the Ephesians reveals how precious Paul's ministry in this city had been. Here in Ephesus the sons of Sceva, trying to copy Paul's miracles, are attacked by the very demon they were attempting to cast out. Here in Ephesus he was again threatened, and Paul departs to go into Greece. From this point we recognize a change in the conduct and ministry of the apostle. He seems to have lost his sense of composure and appears to be driven by a strange urge to go back to Jerusalem. It is hard to understand this obsession to go to Jerusalem, when we realize that his commission was to the Gentiles. It was the Gentile church in Antioch, not the church at Jerusalem, which had sent him forth.

If you will read carefully Acts 20 and 21, you will be impressed with Paul's determination to reach Jerusalem, and as a result he stayed only a short while in each place, and spent less and less time in preaching.

After departing from Greece he stopped at Troas, where he waited for his companions to join him. Here he seems to have preached only one sermon (a long one lasting till midnight). From here Paul goes to Assos, then on to Mitylene, then to Samos, on to Trogyllium, and finally comes to Miletus. He had hoped to stop for a visit to Ephesus but instead he called the elders from Ephesus to Miletus. It is a scene of hurry, hurry, hurry. In only one of the various places he stopped did he take time to preach. And now at Miletus he finds no time to visit Ephesus, less than forty miles away. Why all the hurry, Paul? What is causing this unrest and haste? We have the answer in Acts 20:16,

> For Paul had determined to sail by [past] Ephesus, because he would not spend the time in Asia: for he hasted, if it were possible for him, to be at Jerusalem the day of Pentecost (Acts 20:16).

The important word in this verse is *determined*. Paul *determined* to pass up his work in Asia, in order that he might go where God had strictly forbidden him to go. Paul was commissioned to go to the Gentiles, and to stay away from the city of Jerusalem. As long as Paul stuck to his job of evangelizing the Gentiles all was well, but when Paul became obsessed with the desire to step out of the will of God, and go to the city of Jerusalem, his ministry to the Gentiles comes to an abrupt end, and the apostle of *grace* is to find out that grace does not justify disobedience to the will of the Lord.

In our next message we shall trace the rest of Paul's experience in the closing chapters of Acts, which are occupied almost entirely with Paul's arrest, trial and final imprisonment in Rome.

In closing this message we want to make one practical application. Grace does not give license to disobey God. No matter how sincere we may be, it does not excuse disregard for the clear will of God. And Paul was no exception. Why should the Lord permit the apostle of grace to fall into the trap of legalism after his uncompromising declaration of the unconditional grace of God? Why did the Holy Spirit permit Dr. Luke to record for us the tragic end to Paul's public ministry after his wonderful missionary activities? Why must we be told about this man, who had been so faithful, that he spent his closing days in prison, and was executed for his faith? It is written for our admonition. It is a warning that even the godliest of men (even Paul) is not immune to yielding to the temptation of the flesh, when he takes liberties with the clear and unmistakable warnings of God. Paul knew better, for he himself tells us that the experience of Israel in the wilderness was to teach us that we cannot disobey God and escape God's judgment (I Corinthians 10:1-10) and says,

> Now all these things happened unto them for ensamples: and they are written for our admonition, upon whom the ends of the world [ages] are come.
>
> Wherefore let him that thinketh he standeth take heed lest he fall (I Corinthians 10:11, 12).

CHAPTER TWENTY-TWO

Paul's Belated Testimony

Does our love for others justify our disobedience to God? Is it possible that our motives may be pure and our purposes the highest, and yet be completely out of the will of God? Does sincerity excuse disobedience? We may find the answer to these questions in the experience of Paul toward the end of his third missionary journey. So great was Paul's love for his brethren, the Jews, that it blinded him to the clear commands of his Lord. The final chapters of the book of Acts are largely occupied with Paul's experience in a city where he had been strictly forbidden to spend his time. The city of Jerusalem was "off limits" for the apostle. It was "verboten" by his Master. It was this sincere desire of Paul to preach in Jerusalem to his brethren according to the flesh which brought an untimely end to his ministry, and cut short his missionary activities. Beginning with chapter 20 we have the tragic story of Paul's stubborn disobedience to the will of God. To understand the closing days of Paul after he visited Jerusalem for the last time we must go back to the beginning of Paul's Christian experience.

OUR LORD'S COMMISSION (Acts 1:8)

Our Lord had been very clear in giving His closing instructions to His disciples, and His last words were:

> . . . ye shall be witnesses unto me both in Jerusalem, and in all Judaea, and in Samaria, and unto the uttermost part of the earth (Acts 1:8).

The program was in three stages:

1. Beginning at Jerusalem.
2. Then to Samaria.
3. Then to the nations.

The first seven chapters of Acts, ending with the stoning of Stephen, closed the first step in this program, "to the Jew first." With Philip's journey into Samaria the second step begins; and immediately after this the third step, *to the Gentiles,* beginning with the conversion of the household of Cornelius is inaugurated, and is continuing to this day. After the conversion of the Gentile Cornelius, God ends His dealing with the nation of Israel, Peter's ministry to the Jews disappears, and Paul now takes over. His conversion is recorded in Acts 9. It was the beginning in earnest of the third phase of Christ's commission, "unto the uttermost part of the earth." Paul's part in this ministry was made very plain to him at the beginning. He was to "bear my name before the Gentiles" (Acts 9:15).

After his conversion Paul witnessed to the people in Damascus, but he could not forget about his persecution of the Jewish Christians in Jerusalem, and as a result was seized with an overwhelming irrepressible desire to witness to his own people, the Jews. But that stage was past. The order "to the Jew first" had been fulfilled, and Paul's ministry was not to be to *national* Israel at all, but to the individual sinner, both Jew and Gentile. Of this Paul had been definitely told when he visited Jerusalem soon after his conversion. However, it was not until Paul was arrested and brought to trial at the end of his ministry that he tells us the details of his first visit to Jerusalem. It was during Paul's *last* visit to Jerusalem to face trial in the very place which God warned him to avoid, that he tells us the whole story. While giving his testimony he relates this experience which he had not mentioned before.

> And it came to pass, that, when I was come again to Jerusalem [after his conversion], even while I prayed in the temple, I was in a trance;
> And I saw him [Jesus] saying unto me, Make haste, and *get thee quickly out of Jerusalem:* for they will not receive thy testimony concerning me (Acts 22:17, 18).

The command was clear and definite. *Get out of Jerusalem!* But Paul, instead of obeying without question, offers excuses, and says:

> . . . Lord, they know that I imprisoned and beat in every synagogue them that believed on thee (Acts 22:19).

But the Lord says, "No, Paul, your ministry is not to Israel but to the Gentiles. You have no business in Jerusalem. Jerusalem has been forsaken by Me; it is doomed to be destroyed and its people scattered." God seems to say to Paul, "What are you doing in the Temple? This Temple has been abandoned by Me, the veil has been rent." And in spite of Paul's request that he be allowed to witness in Jerusalem, the Lord says emphatically, *get out of Jerusalem, and stay out!*

> . . . *Depart:* for I will send thee far hence unto the Gentiles (Acts 22:21).

We emphasize and repeat this prohibition against Paul's visiting Jerusalem, for it was his disobedience and disregard of this clear warning that led to his final arrest and imprisonment. Paul did leave Jerusalem, but only with reluctance. He had such a burning love for his fellow Jews that he found it hard to see God's will. We can excuse Paul for visiting Jerusalem the first time, for the Lord had not yet given him this serious warning. But after this unmistakable command to stay out of Jerusalem, there was no excuse for Paul ever returning, for God repeated the warning over and over again. As we touched upon before, the beginning of Paul's downward course was the occasion when he circumcised Timothy in order to pacify the legalists. Paul had preached and defended his gospel of grace, teaching that Gentiles and Jews are saved without circumcision or the works of the law. His compromise in circumcising Timothy was the first step in that which follows.

THE NEXT STEP

The next step in Paul's willful ignoring of God's warning was in the city of Corinth when he takes a legal vow, shaves his head, places himself under law, and determines to visit Jerusalem once more anyway (Acts 18:18-21). When we begin to disobey God, the tendency is for this disobedience to increase and blind us to the folly of our sinful course. We trace this tendency in the incidents recorded in Acts 20.

> And we sailed thence, and came the next day over against Chios; and the next day we arrived at Samos, and tarried at Trogyllium; and the next day we came to Miletus (Acts 20:15).

The next day! The next day! The next day! Three times in one verse we read the expression, *and the next day.* No time to stop and preach in Chios; no time to preach in Samos; no time to tell the Gospel story to the people in Trogyllium; no time for any delay, but hurry, hurry, hurry. Why all this haste? The next verse explains it all:

> For Paul had determined to sail by Ephesus, *because he would not spend the time in Asia:* for *he hasted,* if it were possible for him, to be at Jerusalem the day of Pentecost (Acts 20:16).

What business did Paul have in Jerusalem? He had been told to stay away. What business had the apostle of grace wanting to observe a legal holiday, the day of Pentecost which had already been fulfilled over twenty-five years before? Paul knew all this. He also knew that in Jerusalem he would experience God's disapproval and judgment, for he tells these Ephesian elders:

> And now, behold, I go bound in the spirit unto Jerusalem, not knowing the things that shall befall me there:
> Save that the Holy Ghost witnesseth in every city, saying that bonds and afflictions abide me (Acts 20:22, 23).

We ask the question: if Paul knew all this, why did he insist upon going there? He was going to Jerusalem bound in the spirit, but it was not the Holy Spirit. The word "spirit" in which Paul went to Jerusalem is not written with a capital letter, indicating that it was Paul's spirit which prompted him to go in direct violation of the Holy Spirit's warning. How can we explain Paul's apparent willful disobedience? We repeat that Paul's motive was pure. He was prompted by an all-consuming love for his fellow brethren according to the flesh — the Jews. And so, knowing what the result would be, he nevertheless replies:

> But none of these things move me, neither count I my life dear unto myself, so that I might finish my course with joy, and the ministry, which I have received of the Lord Jesus, to testify the gospel of the grace of God (Acts 20:24).

Notice Paul's determination. He says, "None of these things move me." All the warnings of the Holy Spirit that his going to Jerusalem would result in bonds and afflictions and put an end to his public ministry were disregarded, overshadowed by his determination to have his own way.

ON TO JERUSALEM

We now follow Paul sorrowfully as he leaves the Ephesian elders. They escort him to the dock on his way to imprisonment, knowing they were seeing Paul for the last time here below. As we come to Acts 21, the haste which had gripped Paul had intensified. After leaving Miletus he does not make a single stop until he is forced to wait for seven days at Tyre, because the ship was delayed there for a week unloading and loading her cargo. During his brief stay here (during which time it appears that he did not preach at all — an unusual thing for Paul) he spent just one day at Ptolemais, and came to Caesarea. But before he left Tyre, he was once again reminded of the dangerous course he was pursuing:

> And finding disciples [at Tyre], we tarried there seven days: who said to Paul through the *Spirit* that he should not go up to Jerusalem (Acts 21:4).

Notice the Holy Spirit spoke once more saying, "Paul, don't go to Jerusalem. Change your plans." But Paul was determined and once more disregarded the warning. We marvel at the patience of our Lord. One might have expected the Lord to say, "You have no excuse so I will cease dealing with you. Go ahead and learn your lesson the hard way." But no! The Lord is patient with Paul, and comes next with another roadblock. While tarrying in Caesarea for a number of days (probably debating what he would do), God sent a prophet direct from Jerusalem, the forbidding city, to once more plead with Paul:

> . . . there came down from Judaea a certain prophet named Agabus.
> And when he was come unto us, he took Paul's girdle [belt], and bound his own hands and feet, and said, *Thus saith the Holy Ghost,* So shall the Jews at Jerusalem bind the man that owneth this girdle, and shall deliver him into the hands of the Gentiles (Acts 21:10, 11).

THUS SAITH THE HOLY GHOST

One would think that this final warning, so emphatically given, would have made Paul change his mind. Notice that this prophet Agabus came all the way from *Jerusalem.* All the other previous warnings had been along the way, but this last and final warning came from Jerusalem itself, the city he had been strictly forbid-

den to visit. When the disciples heard this prophecy of Agabus they were greatly disturbed and pleaded with Paul to change
his mind. It is interesting to note that one of those who pled
with Paul was one of his dearest, most devoted friends, Doctor
Luke. This is indicated by the pronoun *we* in the next verse.
Dr. Luke, who was present with the prophet Agabus, also
pleaded with Paul:

> And when *we* [including Luke] heard these things, both
> we [the members of Paul's party], and they of that place,
> besought him not to go up to Jerusalem (Acts 21:12).

Then comes Paul's final declaration. He will not budge in
his determination, in spite of all warnings, and says:

> . . . What mean ye to weep and to break mine heart?
> for I am ready not to be bound only, but also to die at Jeru-
> salem for the name of the Lord Jesus (Acts 21:13).

Somehow one cannot help but admire the wonderful determination and wholehearted devotion and the love for his fellow Jews
which is expressed in these words of Paul. He had set his face
to go to Jerusalem. Not even the Holy Spirit would deter him.
His mind is made up. He will not be swerved from his purpose
even though, it will cost him his life. Why did not the Lord stop
Paul? He could have taken him home to glory or prevented
him in some other way from continuing in his mad determination.
It was because God knew it all before hand, and was going to
demonstrate His abounding grace in making Paul's mistake the
occasion for a great and wonderful ministry after he reached
Rome. Yes, God can cause even the wrath of man to praise Him.
And so in the purpose and plan of God, He overruled Paul's
willfulness and turned it into the greatest ministry of Paul —
the writing of the prison epistles to the churches while he spent
his closing days a "prisoner of the Lord Jesus Christ." Paul
the apostle of grace is to be Exhibit Number One of the overrul-
ing, abounding grace of God, which he so emphatically had declared. It did not excuse Paul, but it does magnify the grace
of God. This we hope to demonstrate in the coming messages.

CHAPTER TWENTY-THREE

The Right Motive—The Wrong Method

From Jerusalem to Rome! This might well be the title of the closing six chapters of the book of Acts. It may also be the caption of the entire book, for the history of Acts begins at Jerusalem and closes in Rome. It begins with Israel in the capital of Palestine, with the gospel of the Kingdom being preached to "the Jew first," and it ends in Rome, the capital of the Gentile world of that day. It was the order our Lord had given in Acts 1:8, "beginning at Jerusalem' and concluding with the Gospel "unto the ends of the earth."

After Paul had ignored the last warning of the prophet Agabus, not to go to Jerusalem, the disciples saw the futility of further efforts at persuading Paul. Significant indeed are the words of these disciples:

> And when he [Paul] would not be persuaded we ceased, saying, The will of the Lord be done (Acts 21:14).

Paul finally reaches Jerusalem, and immediately contacts the apostles there. He declares unto them his wonderful ministry among the Gentiles, and they were glad:

> And when they heard it, they glorified the Lord . . . (Acts 21:20).

But now a serious problem arose and a clever trap is laid for Paul. The disciples feared what the results of Paul's visit might mean, and seeking for a solution and compromise they unconsciously set a trap for Paul. They say,

> Thou seest, brother, how many thousands of Jews there are which believe; and they are all zealous of the law:
> And they are informed of thee, that thou teachest all the

Jews which are among the Gentiles to forsake Moses, saying
that they ought not to circumcise their children, neither to
walk after the customs.
What is it therefore? the multitude must needs come together: for they will hear that thou art come.
Do therefore this that we say to thee: We have four men
which have a vow on them;
Them take, and purify thyself with them [according to
the Law], and be at charges with them, that they may shave
their heads [according to the Law]: and all may know that
those things, whereof they were informed concerning thee,
are nothing [not true]; but that thou thyself also walkest
orderly [legally], and keepest the law (Acts 21:20-24).

THE GREAT CRISIS

Up until now all had gone well, but now a crisis arose. Rumors had come to Jerusalem that Paul had been teaching that
law-keeping had no part in salvation, and that circumcision was
not essential to being saved. What could be done to convince the
multitude that this was not true? Now, of course, the rumors
were true (that was the problem). He had preached the Gospel to Jew and Gentile alike. In that Gospel the law could
not be recognized. Neither law-works nor circumcision have
any part in the plan of salvation. To prevent a riot, a
compromise must be made to pacify the Judaistic legalists.
The disciples in Jerusalem were willing to admit that the
Gentiles were not required to observe the law — but the
Jews — *yes!* They still had a double standard. We must remind
you that they were still in the transition period from Judaism to
Christianity, and the disciples in Jerusalem had accepted the
Lord Jesus Christ, but still held on tenaciously to the Law of
Moses. They were all zealous for the law. They kept all the
ordinances of the law, abstained from certain meats, kept the
feast days, went to the Temple, took legal vows and purified
themselves. They did not yet know that the middle wall of
partition had been completely broken down, and now there
was no difference, but all must be saved by grace and grace
alone. This lesson has not been learned even today by millions of
church members. Paul had made all this very clear when he met
with the disciples in Jerusalem previously. He had clearly stated
his position to Peter twenty years before, as reported by Paul
in Galatians. Peter had to come to Antioch and had entered

fully into the fellowship of the Gentile believers there and had
embraced the liberty they had, without the works of the law.
But then certain of these same legalists who now accuse Paul
had come to Antioch, and Peter withdrew himself from the fellowship of these believers and placed himself back under the
law. Listen to Paul's denunciation of Peter's double standard
— one plan of salvation for the Jew, and another for the Gentile.
We quote as he puts Peter in his place:

> We who are Jews by nature, and not sinners of the Gentiles,
> Knowing that a man is not justified by the works of the
> law, but by the faith of Jesus Christ, even we [Jews] have
> believed in Jesus Christ, that we [Jews] might be justified
> by the faith of Christ, and not by the works of the law:
> for by the works of the law shall no flesh be justified (Gala-
> tians 2:15, 16).

No double standard, Paul had said over twenty years before.
Now at this last visit to Jerusalem we find this same Paul falling into the same trap for which he had rebuked Peter. Peter
compromised to avoid the animosity of the legalists from Jerusalem. Here Paul compromises for the same reason. He was
afraid of his critics — or was he afraid? Upon second thought,
it may not have been fear at all, but an honest conviction, that
a little compromising, a little cutting of corners, would be justified in his eagerness to win these same enemies to Christ. But are
we ever justified in compromising the truth, even though our
motives are the very best? Paul's experience should teach us
the lesson. Before we see the result we remind you that all of
their accusations against Paul were *true*, and Paul in denying
it was not to be excused, no matter how honest his motive.

THE LAST STRAW

So Paul, prompted by the best of motives, bows to the suggestion:

> Then Paul took the men, and the next day purifying him-
> self with them entered into the temple, to signify the accomp-
> lishment of the days of purification, until that an offering
> should be offered for every one of them (Acts 21:26).

It is difficult to imagine Paul going back to the law, after his
valiant defense of grace for thirty years. What a strange sight
to see the apostle of grace, Paul, back in the Temple which had

been abandoned by the Lord, going through dead ceremonies, legal rituals, and offering a sacrifice, after Christ had made the one sacrifice once for all. There is no mention of prayer or seeking the direction of the Holy Spirit. There was no waiting upon the Lord; in fact, there was no occasion to wait, for the Lord's will had been clearly made known before. In his own soul Paul knew that all the rituals, ceremonies, special days and offerings, as well as the law itself, had been fulfilled in Christ. The ordinances to which he now turned again had been nailed to the cross. While he felt justified in his compromising because he considered it the only way to appease his accusers, he was to find this utterly fruitless; for instead of quieting his enemies, it turned out to do the very opposite. "Peace at any price" was not the answer then, nor is it today. But Paul missed his golden opportunity. To the suggestion of these compromising disciples Paul could have stated his convictions and stood his ground as he had done in Antioch when Peter visited him.

THE UPROAR IN JERUSALEM

Instead of asserting his convictions, he yields to the temptation and goes to the Temple to indicate that he was a good Jew and kept the law. But it was of no avail. We quote here the result:

> And when the seven days were almost ended, the Jews which were of Asia, when they saw him [Paul] in the temple, stirred up all the people, and laid hands on him,
>
> Crying out, Men of Israel, help: This is the man, that teacheth all men every where against the people, and the law, and this place: and further brought Greeks [unclean Gentiles] also into the temple, and hath polluted this holy place.
>
> And all the city was moved, and the people ran together: and they took Paul, and drew [dragged] him out of the temple: and forthwith the doors were shut.
>
> And as they went about to kill him, tidings came unto the chief captain of the band, that all Jerusalem was in an uproar.
>
> Who immediately took soldiers and centurions, and ran down unto them: and when they saw the chief captain and soldiers, they left beating of Paul.
>
> Then the chief captain came near, and took him, and commanded him to be bound with two chains; and demanded who he was, and what he had done (Acts 21:27, 28, 30-33).

Paul's good intentions landed him in jail. Paul's public ministry is ended, and the rest of the story in Acts is a record of Paul's trial, his journey to Rome, and ends with Paul in prison. All his efforts at appeasement, compromise, concession and cooperation were of no avail.

Paul's noble intentions blew up in his face; the evil suggestion of compromise by the disciples resulted in apparent failure from beginning to end. Thinking that compromise was the way to peace, it ended in a riot. The object they sought was not reached. I wonder what went through the mind of Paul as the mob threatened to kill him, and when heavy chains were placed upon him. He must have remembered the words of our Lord at his first visit to Jerusalem, "Depart, for they will not receive thy testimony concerning me." Undoubtedly the words of Agabus in Caesarea must have rung in his ears, "So shall the Jews at Jerusalem bind the man that owneth this girdle" (Acts 21:11).

So violent was the attack upon Paul that the soldiers had to carry him, to protect him from the violence of the people. As they carried him up the stairs into the castle, he asks permission to speak to the people, which was granted, once he was out of reach of the mob. The next chapter (Acts 22) records his speech which was Paul's own testimony of his conversion, and in the course of his testimony he relates how he had been warned at that time to stay out of Jerusalem. It must have been a difficult and humiliating thing for Paul to relate the incident, now that he is in custody as a result of his deliberate disobedience to God's command,

> . . . Make haste, and get thee quickly out of Jerusalem: for they will not receive thy testimony concerning me (Acts 22:18).

It took many years for Paul to learn that God meant what He said, but what a painful way to find it out.

Lessons for Us

Why did the Holy Spirit have all this recorded, instead of casting the mantle of charitable silence over the whole record of failure? It is recorded for our warning and admonition. Paul tells us that the failures of Israel which provoked God's displeasure and brought God's chastening were recorded as warnings to us. He says,

> Now all these things happened unto them for ensamples:
> and they are written for our admonition . . . (I Corinthians
> 10:11).

In the same way Paul's record of dismal failure is also written to remind us that the saintliest of saints can fall when they
act in the energy of the flesh, instead of obeying the Lord. The
lessons we may learn from Paul's experience are numberless.
First, we repeat, the Bible was not written to exalt human nature even in the godliest of men, but rather to exalt the grace
of God. If Paul was not immune to the danger of acting in self-
will, how much ought we to be on constant guard! Second, our
own conscience, no matter how sincere, is not a safe guide when
it is in conflict with the clear teachings of Scripture. Third, we
may learn that God's people are not spared the rod when walk-
ing in self-will and disobedience. There is an awful price attached to disobedience, for Paul had to spend the rest of
his life in prison. And then another lesson lies hidden here. We
see the matchless grace of God, for the Lord did not cast aside
Paul because of his defection; in infinite grace He overruled
it all and made Paul's years in confinement the occasion for the
greatest of blessing, for the seven prison epistles were written
for the Church during his imprisonment.

Finally, here is a solemn warning against compromising the
Gospel. It did not win over his enemies; it did not pacify his
accusers. There are many today who believe that a pure, sincere
motive is an excuse for relaxing the truth of the Gospel. We
are living in an ecumenical age of compromise and we should ask
ourselves, How far are we justified in adapting our methods to
gain a noble end? How far can we go in soliciting the fellowship
of the enemies of the Gospel, because we feel we can win them by
such compromise? These are important questions. May God give
us a spirit of discernment and show us that the place of disobedience is "without the camp, bearing his reproach" (Hebrews
13:13).

CHAPTER TWENTY-FOUR

From Jerusalem to Rome

There is nothing more cruel than religious hatred and bigotry. More atrocious crimes have been committed in the name of religion than in any other. The world of the ungodly is often more fair and just than many of those who profess to represent the love of God. I would ten times rather be tried by a secular, civil court than by a religious tribunal. In religious controversies too often the accusers act also as judges and jury. In world courts no verdict is ever reached until both sides have been heard, and the proceedings have been legal. Yes, let me fall into the hands of ungodly men rather than in the hands of religious bigots. It was ever thus. One can not but feel his blood boil as he reads the wholly illegal and immoral trial of Jesus before His accusers at His crucifixion. He was illegally arrested, illegally condemned, and given an illegal trial before the religious Sanhedrin. If they could, they would have murdered Him without a trial, but they dared not because they had no authority to do so. So they delivered Him to Pilate who sought diligently to free Jesus and would have done so, were it not for fear of a riot by the religious mob of blood-thirsty sadists, led by the members of the ruling religious Sanhedrin and the "super-pious" Pharisees. If the heathen Pilate could, he would have released Jesus but religious pressure made him yield.

THE SAME WITH PAUL

The arrest and trial of Paul the Apostle and follower of Jesus, tells again the same story. The treatment he received from his religious accusers was without mercy, while the civil authorities sought for every means to discharge Paul. It is interesting to trace this in your Bible. After Paul was seized in the Temple (Acts 21:27) he was manhandled by the bigoted religious mob; and without a hearing or a trial or a chance to defend himself, they attempted to kill him, but he was rescued by a Gentile pagan captain. Here is the record:

> And as they went about to kill him, tidings came unto the chief captain of the band, that all Jerusalem was in an uproar.
>
> Who immediately took soldiers and centurions, and ran down unto them: and when they saw the chief captain and the soldiers, they left beating of Paul (Acts 21:31, 32).

Attacked by a religious mob — saved by an ungodly captain. This ungodly captain permitted Paul to state his case and address his persecutors. We repeat, there is nothing more cruel and merciless with blind hate and injustice than religious bigotry. I am not referring to born-again believers, but professing, unregenerate Christendom, as well as other religions. Paul accepted the opportunity to defend himself before his accusers, but under guard of the civil authorities. His defense is recorded in Acts 22. After the chief captain had heard Paul, he took the chains from his hands and feet and arranged to give him another opportunity to state his case the next day. Paul accepts the challenge to once more face his religious enemies, under the protection of the civil powers. But the result was the same. The frenzied crowd of fanatical religious formalists interrupted Paul and threatened to kill him then and there. Once again Paul is rescued from his religious enemies by ungodly soldiers:

> And when there arose a great dissension, the chief captain, fearing lest Paul should have been pulled in pieces of them, commanded the soldiers to go down, and to take him by force from among them, and to bring him into the castle (Acts 23:10).

That night Paul received a visit from his Master. The Lord knew that Paul could bear no more without definite help. The Lord knew the worst was yet to come for Paul, and so prepared him in advance:

> And the night following the Lord stood by him, and said, Be of good cheer, Paul: for as thou hast testified of me in Jerusalem, so must thou bear witness also at Rome (Acts 23:11).

Here Paul receives the assurance his enemies will not be able
to kill him. And how he needed this assurance, for at that very
moment a plot was being hatched to kill Paul:

> And when it was day, certain of the Jews banded together,
> and bound themselves under a curse, saying that they would
> neither eat nor drink till they had killed Paul (Acts 23:12).

To get their hands on Paul, they requested that he be brought
forth for a simple hearing and they would pounce upon him and
kill him (Acts 23:14, 15). How relentless the acrimony of the
religious zealots of the law in their hatred for the apostle of
grace! But God foiled their plans and used a nephew of Paul
to thwart this diabolical conspiracy. Somehow this little fellow
overheard the plot and came and told Paul, who in turn informed one of the sentries. The lad was then brought to the chief
captain who was willing to listen to his story. How wonderfully
the Lord looks after His own. We do not know the boy's name,
but the Lord knew and used him. After telling the captain what
he knew about the plot,

> . . . the chief captain then let the young man depart, and
> charged him, See thou tell no man that thou hast shewed
> these things to me (Acts 23:22).

FROM JERUSALEM TO ROME

Paul is therefore taken secretly out of Jerusalem and sent to
Caesarea to be placed under the protection of the governor,
Felix. Paul now leaves Jerusalem, driven out by the very people
he had so greatly yearned to bring to Christ. This is the end of
Paul's desire to witness in Jerusalem. As Paul is spirited away
under guard of two hundred soldiers and seventy cavalrymen,
and two hundred spearmen, late at night under cover of darkness, his mind must have gone back to that day many years before
when the Lord had said to Paul as he prayed in the Temple in
Jerusalem,

> . . . Make haste, and get thee quickly out of Jerusalem: for
> they will not receive thy testimony concerning me (Acts
> 22:18).

He must have remembered how he argued with the Lord about
his desire to bring the Gospel to his brethren according to the
flesh, and how the Lord said to him:

... Depart: for I will send thee far hence unto the Gentiles (Acts 22:21).

How Paul must have been reminded that what he was now suffering was the result of his disobedience to this warning of God and his stubborn insistence upon going to Jerusalem anyway. We believe Paul had finally learned his lesson. From what follows in Acts 25, it is evident that every desire to go to Jerusalem, every urge to witness to his fellow Israelites there was completely taken away from Paul. As he left Jerusalem under heavy guard he knew his ministry to the Jews was coming to an end, and he at last became reconciled to it all. He had expressed the desire to visit Rome, but how little he knew it would be as a prisoner in chains.

PAUL BEFORE FELIX

After Paul arrived in Caesarea, he was placed by Felix in Herod's judgment hall. But even though Jerusalem had been left behind by Paul, his accusers from Jerusalem followed him. Five days after Paul arrived in Caesarea, a band of his religious persecutors led by Ananias the high priest came to Caesarea. Among them may have been some of the forty men who had taken the oath neither to eat nor drink till they had killed Paul. I often wonder what happened to these forty men. Did they stick to their vow to either die of starvation or kill Paul? If they kept their vow, they must have starved to death, but I would rather imagine they gave in after missing a few meals.

Once more Paul is faced with his accusers from Jerusalem. The high priest had brought along a high-powered, glib-tongued lawyer named Tertullus. His accusation was that Paul was

... a pestilent fellow, and a mover of seditions among all the Jews throughout the world, and a ringleader of the sect of the Nazarenes (Acts 24:5).

Once more Paul defends himself as he addresses Felix, who dismisses him, only to call him back a second time. Intending to hear him again at a later date (which evidently he did — v. 26), the last we hear of Felix is that he

... trembled, and answered, Go thy way for this time; when I have a convenient season, I will call for thee (Acts 24:25).

Two years later Felix' term of office expired and Porcius Festus became governor in his place, but Felix seeking the favor of Paul's enemies did nothing about Paul. Luke significantly adds:

> But after two years Porcius Festus came into Felix' room: and Felix, willing to shew the Jews a pleasure, left Paul bound (Acts 24:27).

THE SILENT YEARS

The Holy Spirit has cast a complete mantle of silence over these two years which Paul spent in prison in Caesarea. What Paul did during those two years we do not know, but we may be sure he had much time to meditate and think over the turbulent years of his Christian experience. It was very probable during these two years that Paul was finally convinced his ministry was not in Jerusalem, and he is finally ready to admit that his Lord was right when He warned Paul to stay out of that city. Here he was imprisoned in Caesarea, all because he would not heed the repeated warnings of the Holy Spirit. This is evident, we believe, from the record in Acts 25.

After two years in prison, Felix the governor was replaced by Festus who made a political trip to the city of Jerusalem. With the new governor in their city, Paul's enemies from Jerusalem made one more attempt to lay their hands on him, and requested that the governor permit them to bring Paul back to Jerusalem for trial in order that they might kill him on the way (Acts 25:1-3). However, Festus refused the request and instead invited Paul's enemies to come to Caesarea. Once again we see the hypocrisy of religion, for the civil heathen governor was kinder to Paul than these religious bigots. Finally Festus yields to the pressure to take Paul to Jerusalem for trial and asks Paul,

> . . . Wilt thou go up to Jerusalem, and there be judged of these things before me? (Acts 25:9).

THE APPEAL TO CAESAR

To our surprise Paul refuses to return to Jerusalem. He realizes for the final time that the Lord meant what He said when He warned: "Paul, stay away from Jerusalem; don't go near the place, for they will not receive your testimony there." He is at last through with his desire to go to the forbidden city, and so in order to escape being sent to Jerusalem he appeals to Caesar and demands that he be sent to Rome instead.

> Then said Paul, I stand at Caesar's judgment seat, where I ought to be judged. . . .
> . . . I appeal unto Caesar (Acts 25:10, 11).

As a Roman citizen Paul had the right to appeal to the high court of the Roman empire. Paul knew he could not get a fair trial in Jerusalem. His appeal was accepted, and Festus replies,

> . . . Hast thou appealed unto Caesar? unto Caesar shalt thou go (Acts 25:12).

The balance of Acts 25 records Paul's address before King Agrippa who had come for a visit to Festus. After hearing Paul speak, he was convinced of his innocence, but because he had appealed to Caesar he must be sent to Rome for trial. We recommend that the reader carefully study Paul's address before Agrippa as recorded in Acts 26, at the close of which we have the verdict of both Festus and Agrippa.

> And when they were gone aside, they talked between themselves, saying, This man doeth nothing worthy of death or of bonds.
> Then said Agrippa unto Festus, This man might have been set at liberty, if he had not appealed unto Caesar (Acts 26: 31, 32).

The end of the road is in sight, From Jerusalem to Rome is the content of the last two chapters of Acts. The trip to Rome was in full keeping with Paul's own stormy career. He is shipwrecked, cast upon a small island and ends up in the Roman prison.

Before we close this chapter we must again point out the cruelty of religion without Christ. We repeat, there is nothing as cruel, merciless and wicked as religious bigotry. When Paul was saved he was not saved from a life of overt sin but the sin of *religion*. Someone has said, "Christ came to save men from two things, *sin* and *religion*, and the worst of these is religion without Christ." Cain was very religious but he murdered his brother. Saul was religious, fanatically religious and zealous, but he persecuted the Church. My friend, are you saved? or just religious? Jesus said to a most religious man, Nicodemus, *ye must be born again.*

CHAPTER TWENTY-FIVE

God's Mysterious Dealing

> God moves in a mysterious way,
> His wonders to perform.
> He plants His footsteps in the sea,
> And rides upon the storm.
>
> Blind unbelief is sure to err,
> And say His work is vain.
> God is His own interpreter,
> And He will make it plain.

The Apostle Paul said in Romans 8:28,

> And we know that all things work together for good to them that love God, to them who are the called according to his purpose.

We wonder if Paul realized that he himself was one of the most outstanding examples of this inspired statement. From the human standpoint Paul's life was a failure. If Paul lived today he would be branded a fanatic, a jailbird and a crank, probably even a fundamentalist. He was in trouble all the time, and his public ministry was ended during the very prime of his life. In stubborn disobedience to a clear command to stay away from Jerusalem, Paul had insisted on going anyway. Finally, after many warnings, the Lord permitted him to be taken captive and he was compelled to spend the most vigorous years of his life in prison in Jerusalem, Caesarea and Rome. It did seem that the end of Paul's life was to be one of complete failure. But "God moves in a mysterious way, His wonders to perform." For God was able to overrule the mistake of Paul, and by His matchless grace the closing years of Paul's life became the most fruitful of his entire career, even though in prison.

How long Paul was held prisoner in Rome before he was executed we do not know. There are some who teach that Paul was released and made another missionary journey and went to Spain and even preached the Gospel in Britain. This of course is mere conjecture, and someday we shall know. But one thing we do know, that the book of Acts closes with Paul a prisoner in Rome. For his activities after his arrival in Rome we must go to the prison epistles which furnish us with a volume of information concerning Paul during the closing years of his life.

THE SEVEN PRISON EPISTLES

It was during the time Paul spent in Rome as the "prisoner of Christ" that he gave to the Church her "Magna Charta." These seven epistles are Ephesus, Philippians, Colossians, II Timothy, Titus, Philemon and Hebrews. We should have known very little about the great doctrines of the Church and the organization, order and discipline of the Church in this dispensation were it not for the instructions given to Paul by special revelation, and recorded in these seven important documents. There is no measuring of the importance of Paul's ministry while in prison. Writing from his prison in Rome, Paul wrote to the Philippian Christians:

> But I would ye should understand, brethren, that the things which happened unto me have fallen out rather unto the furtherance of the gospel;
>
> So that my bonds in Christ are manifest in all the palace, and in all other places;
>
> And many of the brethren in the Lord, waxing confident by my bonds, are much more bold to speak the word without fear (Philippians 1:12-14).

These words were written while Paul was a prisoner in Rome and were addressed to the church in Philippi, where Paul had experienced his first imprisonment. He must have been thinking of that night when he and Silas sang and prayed, and the Lord sent the earthquake and the prison doors were opened unto them. Paul must have remembered the conversion of the jailor and his family. Humanly speaking this whole family would never have been saved were it not for Paul's imprisonment. And now as

he recalls how God had turned seeming tragedy into great blessing, and made the wrath of man the means of salvation for a
whole household, he could see that in all his afflictions an un-
seen hand was directing his life.

Now he is again a prisoner in Rome and he must have been
meditating upon that experience many years ago. He is now to
re-experience the same thing in an even greater measure. From
man's standpoint Paul's arrest and incarceration was the end of
his ministry, but instead God made it a wide open door for His
willing servant. In Philippi he had had a jail service, unlike
any before or since. It was at midnight, as they prayed and
sang. In the narrative Dr. Luke adds a significant phrase which
is easily overlooked:

> And at midnight Paul and Silas prayed, and sang praises
> unto God: *and the prisoners heard them* (Acts 16:25).

And the prisoners heard them! Why did Dr. Luke add that
phrase, "and the prisoners heard them"? It was probably in
order to let us know how impressed these prisoners were by the
testimony of these two men; for although all the prison doors
were opened, and everyone's bands were loosed, not one tried
to escape. What an opportunity for these prisoners to flee the
prison with all the handcuffs and chains loose and every door
wide open! No doubt the testimonies of these singing prisoners
had touched their hearts, and instead of running away they
gathered around these two strange men and probably witnessed
the conversion of the jailor. God overruled the wrath of man
and used it for His glory.

That experience in Philippi is now repeated in Rome in a
different but a wider way. Paul says about this that:

> . . . the things which happened unto me have fallen out
> rather unto the futherance of the gospel;
>
> So that my bonds in Christ are manifest in *all the palace,*
> and in all other places (Philippians 1:12, 13).

Here we can read a great deal between the lines without
violating the text. Paul evidently witnessed and testified to
everyone in Caesar's palace. How he found opportunity to do
this is not recorded. Maybe Caesar himself gave Paul an opportunity to witness to his family, and many of them were saved
as a result. This is strongly implied in the conclusion of Paul's

letter to the Philippians. In closing his letter (written in prison) he says:

All the saints salute you, *chiefly they that are of Caesar's household.* (Philippians 4:22).

The ministry of Paul in prison extended even farther, for he adds that his bonds in Christ were manifest not only in all the palace (of Caesar) but also

IN ALL OTHER PLACES

While Paul was a prisoner in Rome he was a world-wide missionary. As a prisoner he was under constant guard. Luke tells us,

And when we came to Rome, the centurion delivered the prisoners to the captain of the guard . . . (Acts 28:16).

These guards were on duty twenty-four hours of the day, probably working in shifts of six or eight hours. Consequently Paul had at least four different soldiers guarding him each day, and how he must have witnessed to them. The guards were Roman soldiers who with Caesar's army were deployed to every part of the Roman Empire and able to bear the message they had heard from Paul to the limits of the Empire. This will explain the problem of how the Gospel reached Spain, Britain, and other parts of Europe after Paul's public ministry ceased. In his letter to the Colossians, Paul tells that the Gospel had "come in all the world" (Colossians 1:6).

How it must have cheered Paul who so much desired to preach the Gospel to the ends of the earth, to know that God had a way of His own to accomplish this purpose. From Paul's prison house in Rome a veritable stream of missionaries poured forth into all the world. Instead of being just *one* missionary, he was allowed to establish a missionary training school in his own private dwelling (Acts 28:16-24).

PAUL'S WRITTEN MINISTRY

The most important and far-reaching ministry of Paul, however, was in the writing of the immortal prison epistles. These were addressed particularly to the Christians in the various countries Paul and others had visited. Paul had established the churches in Ephesus and Philippi. A church had also been formed in Colosse. In his epistles to these three churches he gives the revelation of God concerning the Church without which Christianity could never have continued. It is through Paul that we know that the Church is not an organization or a political party or a society for social reform, but an organism, the Body of Christ, of which Jesus is the Head. To Paul we owe the unfolding of the great doctrines of the Church, her nature, her mission and her destiny. To Paul in particular was committed the revelation of the Rapture and the Second Coming and the full development of the doctrine of the grace of God. And all this is given to us in the epistles which he wrote from Rome while a prisoner, and which we might not have had were it not for the seemingly untimely end of Paul's ministry.

The apostle came to realize this. He learned that God has a plan and that plan is always best. It may be completely contrary to our plans, and we may rebel and grieve, but God knows best. This is the lesson the life of Paul in the book of Acts would teach us. From our restricted and limited understanding, it seemed a tragedy when Paul's marvelous public ministry ended in a prison in Rome, but it was God's way of blessing the Church of all ages through this prison ministry. What an evidence of the grace of God! We remind you again that Paul spent his last days in prison because of his stubborn disobedience to the revealed will of God. God had so definitely warned Paul to stay away from Jerusalem, but Paul had insisted on going. Finally the Lord put an end to his obstinate refusal to heed His warnings, by locking him up in a prison in Rome, so he could not go back to Jerusalem.

I am deeply conscious that this estimate of Paul is vigorously opposed, and many try to defend Paul as though he were infallible. However, Paul was a man of like passions as we are and could say "by the grace of God I am what I am." Paul was the last person to claim infallibility. He knew that in himself, that is in his flesh, there dwelt no good thing. Paul was the great exponent of the grace of God, and God chose to set up Paul as an outstanding example of that very grace.

All we need to do is remember that the Bible was not written to exalt man, but to exhibit the grace of God. And this is the reason the Bible is so seemingly severe in recording the sins of the saintliest and godliest of men that "no flesh should glory in His presence." The tendency to canonize the great men of the

Bible has too often closed our eyes to the "sins" of the saints. Antiquity, tradition and superstition have too often woven a halo and an aura of perfection about the heads of the saints of Scripture so that most Christians shudder at the thought of "criticizing" the heroes of faith. They are considered so far superior that we have sainted them and speak of them as Saint Matthew, Saint Paul, Saint Luke, etc., whereas every believer is a saint. A saint is a *sinner saved by the grace of God.*

The Bible does not make the mistake we so often make. When speaking of our friends we exalt their virtues, but when speaking of our enemies we try to exaggerate their vices. The Bible is not so; it is unbiased, unprejudiced, fair, just, honest, in showing that the best of men by nature are corrupt, lost, and all their righteousness but dross in God's sight, and therefore all stand in need of the grace of God. Paul was no exception. Yet God is able to take our faults and errors, and in His infinite, sovereign purpose brings blessing into our lives in spite of our mistakes. This does not justify our sin and error, but it exalts the grace of God. The brethren of Joseph were wicked and their potential murder of their brother was wholly without excuse or justification, but *a sovereign* God did overrule it for their own salvation. The death of Christ was murder, and seemed like the tragic end of an innocent life, but God used that very death of His Son to bring life to those who deserved death. Oh, the grace, the matchless grace, the wondrous, marvelous grace of God, grace that was greater than all our sin! Thank you, Paul, for not only expounding the grace of God but also for being the great example of that grace.

CHAPTER TWENTY-SIX

Recapitulation

When I was a lad I was exposed to some powerful preaching by old-fashioned preachers whom I shall never forget. Most of what I heard has been forgotten, but one thing I remember is that almost all the sermons followed a more or less regular homiletical pattern. The sermons usually lasted over an hour, and I could tell (without a watch) about how much longer the minister would preach by observing which point in the sermon he had reached. The order was first the introduction – the setting and context of the passage under consideration. Then came point number one with three sub-points; then point or division number two, again with three sub-divisions; and then the same for point number three. This was followed invariably by a recapitulation or review of the entire sermon, and it closed with the "toepassing" or application. The part of the sermon that I was most interested in was the *recapitulation*. It was a brief summing up of all the points covered. I liked it for two reasons: (1) I knew how far along we were; and (2) it helped to fix in my mind what had been preached. It was a good clincher for the whole sermon.

As we come to the end of our study of the book of Acts, I want to follow this pattern and give a review or summary of the material covered. The book of Acts begins in Jerusalem and it closes in Rome. It begins with the ministry of Peter and ends with the ministry of Paul. It begins with the nation of Israel; it ends with the Church, the Body of Christ. It gives us in the first chapter the last commission of our Lord, and also the outline of the book itself, as well as the program for this entire age. The last orders our Lord gave were:

> But ye shall receive power, after that the Holy Ghost is come upon you: and ye shall be witnesses unto me both in Jerusalem, and in all Judaea, and in Samaria, and unto the uttermost part of the earth (Acts 1:8).

The book records the transition from Judaism to Christianity, the revelation of the new program for the Church, an unknown mystery not revealed until after Pentecost. All the Old Testament prophets had foretold and predicted that when Messiah came He would come to the nation of Israel, would deliver her from the bondage of Gentile dominion, set up the Messianic Kingdom, and restore Israel as a nation to its former glory. The Old Testament prophets knew nothing about this Church Age. They knew nothing about the setting aside of the nation and the postponement of the Kingdom. When John the Baptist came he expected Jesus to be the Messiah and so his message to the nation was:

> . . . Repent ye: for the kingdom of heaven is at hand (Matthew 3:2).

This too was the expectation of the disciples who were commanded to limit their message to the nation of Israel exclusively (Matthew 10:5, 6), and brought the same message, "the kingdom of heaven is at hand" (Matthew 10:7). Even as late as the day of the Ascension the disciples were still expecting the Kingdom to be ushered in and asked their last question before Jesus left them,

> . . . wilt thou at this time restore again the kingdom to Israel? (Acts 1:6).

In the foreknown plan of God, the Messiah was to be rejected by the nation, and as a result the Kingdom was to be postponed, the nation of Israel was to be set aside, and in the interim, during this time of the postponement of the Kingdom, God would reveal the "mystery" of the Kingdom, the calling out from among the Gentiles a people for His Name, called the Church and the Body of Christ.

THIS WAS A MYSTERY

Although the rejection of the Messiah by Israel and their setting aside was clearly prophesied in the Old Testament by the prophets, they did not see the secret plan of God called the "mystery which hath been hid from ages and from generations"

(Colossians 1:26). This new revelation of the mystery came as a great shock to the Jews of that day, and it is no wonder it was so difficult to receive the new message of grace. They were expecting the Kingdom and were hardly ready to accept the Gentiles on an equal footing. Even the prophets who prophesied of this mystery age did not understand their own words. Peter tells us plainly and says that they,

> . . . inquired and searched diligently, who prophesied of the grace that should come unto you:
>
> Searching what, or what manner of time the Spirit of Christ which was in them did signify, when it testified beforehand the *sufferings* of Christ, and the *glory* that should follow (I Peter 1:10, 11).

They saw the suffering and they saw the glory but did not know that they were two different events separated by an age of grace (which age has already lasted 1900 years).

God answered their eager questioning concerning this by revealing that "not unto themselves (the kingdom people), but unto us (the Church Age) they did minister the things, which are *now* reported unto you" (I Peter 1:12).

PAUL'S TESTIMONY

Concerning this present Church Age, between the suffering and the glory, Paul says that:

> . . . by revelation he [God] made known unto me the mystery (Ephesians 3:3).

Concerning this mystery he continues:

> Which in other ages was not made known unto the sons of men, as it is now revealed unto his holy apostles and prophets by the Spirit:
>
> That the Gentiles should be fellowheirs, and of the same body, and partakers of his promise in Christ by the gospel (Ephesians 3:5, 6).

THE MYSTERY

The mystery was that Christ would not only come to redeem Israel, but by His death also become the Redeemer of the world, and then after that He would set up the Kingdom. The "mystery of the kingdom of heaven" refers then to this present dispensation; while Jesus is in Heaven, Israel is dispersed out of her land, and the Church is being called out. It is called a mystery because it was unknown before, and also because it is still a mystery to all except believers in the Lord Jesus Christ.

Although this mystery was unknown until after Pentecost, it was not unknown to God, for it was part of His plan which for reasons known to Himself alone He was not pleased to reveal before. There was no possibility of the nation receiving their Messiah when He came the first time. All the prophets had foretold that when Messiah came He would not be received. If they therefore had accepted the offer of the Kingdom, the Old Testament prophets would have been mistaken. In the fore-knowledge of God He had so planned that Christ should be re-jected. This was foretold and it could therefore not be other-wise. The prophet Isaiah had written hundreds of years before:

> Go, and tell this people, Hear ye indeed, but understand not; and see ye indeed, but perceive not,
> Make the heart of this people fat, and make their ears heavy, and shut their eyes; lest they see with their eyes, and hear with their ears, and understand with their heart, and con-vert, and be healed (Isaiah 6:9, 10).

The Lord said He would see to it that Israel would not receive the message. Jesus quotes this very passage when explaining why He spoke in parables. He said,

> Therefore speak I to them in parables: because they seeing see not; and hearing they hear not, neither do they under-stand.
> And in them is fulfilled the prophecy of Esaias, which saith, By hearing ye shall hear, and shall not understand; and seeing ye shall see, and shall not perceive (Matthew 13:13, 14).

Here then we have the real reason for Israel rejecting their Messiah. It was all in God's plan and could not be otherwise. Jesus Himself says concerning this secret plan of God in the mystery,

> But though he had done so many miracles before them, yet they believed not on him (John 12:37).

Why didn't they believe? The answer is unmistakable:

> That the saying of Esaias the prophet might be fulfilled, which he spake, Lord, who hath believed our report? and to whom hath the arm of the Lord been revealed?
> Therefore *they could not believe* (John 12:38, 39).

Notice these words — Therefore they could not believe, because Isaiah said they *would not*, and so the verse in its entirety reads:

Therefore they *could not believe,* because that Esaias said again,

He [God] hath blinded their eyes, and hardened their heart; that they should not see with their eyes, nor understand with their heart, and be converted, and I should heal them.

These things said Esaias, when he saw his glory, and spake of him (John 12:39-41).

No Surprise to God

However, this was all according to plan. God had so ordered it from eternity, and therefore all the prophets had foretold it. God planned it all. This is stated over and over again. Jesus knew this. He said,

And as Moses lifted up the serpent in the wilderness, even so *must* the Son of man be lifted up (John 3:14).

Or listen to Peter on the day of Pentecost as he addresses the Jews at Jerusalem:

Ye men of Israel, hear these words; Jesus of Nazareth, a a man approved of God among you by miracles and wonders and signs, which God did by him in the midst of you, as ye yourselves also know:

Him, being delivered by the *determinate counsel* and *foreknowledge of God,* ye have taken, and by wicked hands have *crucified and slain* (Acts 2:22, 23).

Peter says that the crucifixion of Jesus at the hands of the men of Israel was according to the *determinate counsel and foreknowledge of God.*

We repeat, therefore, the mystery·of the Kingdom of Heaven was this present Church Age, during which the Kingdom nation is set aside, the Kingdom postponed until the Bride of Christ is complete, and then the Messiah will return; He will restore the Kingdom to Israel, and all the prophecies will be fulfilled, and the Kingdom of Heaven — the reign of Heaven's King on earth — will be fully realized. The Kingdom of Heaven is the literal kingdom of Christ on earth. The "mystery of the Kingdom" is the postponement of the Kingdom and the calling out of the Church.

It is the book of Acts which records for us then the transition from this Kingdom program to God's secret purpose in calling out the Church. This is the closing testimony of Paul in the last chapter of Acts. Upon his arrival in Rome he first contacts the Jews in the city and once more proclaims the message of grace, and significantly quotes from Isaiah to explain the rejection of the nation, the postponement of the Kingdom, and the calling out of the Church.

We conclude this series on the great transition book of Acts with the record of Luke in Acts 28. Paul calls the representatives of the Jews in Rome to his quarters and once more offers the invitation and then we read:

> And when they agreed not among themselves, they departed, after that Paul had spoken one word, Well spake the Holy Ghost by Esaias the prophet unto our fathers.
>
> Saying, Go unto this people, and say, Hearing ye shall hear, and shall not understand; and seeing ye shall see, and not perceive:
>
> For the heart of this people is waxed gross, and their ears are dull of hearing, and their eyes have they closed; lest they should see with their eyes, and hear with their ears, and understand with their heart, and should be converted, and I should heal them.
>
> Be it known therefore unto you, that the salvation of God is sent unto the Gentiles, and that they will hear it (Acts 28:25-28).

In this closing verse of the book of Acts we have summed up God's program for this dispensation. While Israel as a nation is set aside, God is building His Church from all peoples, and *after this He will return* to deal once more with Israel and fulfill all the Kingdom promises when

> Christ shall have dominion
> Over land and sea
> Earth's remotest region
> Shall His empire be.

Even so, come, Lord Jesus (Revelation 22:20).

Appendix

For a period of six months the Radio Bible Class released this series of messages based on the book of Acts with special emphasis on the experience of Pentecost. During this time we received thousands, yes, literally hundreds of thousands of letters from our listeners giving us their reaction to these expositions. Among these were, as we anticipated, some who violently disagreed with us in our interpretation. These critical and sometimes condemnatory letters were appreciated for they gave us a better understanding of the thinking and the approach of others to this matter of Pentecost, the baptism in the Holy Spirit, speaking in tongues, etc. For all these letters (even some abusive ones) we are grateful.

At the conclusion of these studies, this was our evaluation of the result of these broadcasts. Two things stand out very clearly. First, these messages were desperately needed and divinely timed. Thousands wrote us to tell how confused they were by the many contradictory reports of Pentecostal experiences. Surely a clarification was needed, and uncounted numbers wrote to thank us for getting them straightened out and settling their doubts. The second thing we learned from the letters was the *cause of this confusion*. Much of it was misunderstanding. It was a result of *not* distinguishing between the baptism *in* the Spirit and the *filling with* the Spirit. People wrote to tell us of their experience of receiving Holy Spirit baptism, when it was not a baptism at all, but a *filling* which they described and experienced.

Once we clear up the misunderstanding between baptism and filling, much of our confusion will be solved. No doubt many of our listeners who wrote in *did have* a definite experience of blessing but were all mixed up on what it really was, and many were unable to distinguish between that which was of the Spirit

and what was merely of the flesh and the emotions. In these
closing words we make one more attempt to clear up the confusion over baptism and filling. They are entirely different experiences. Every born again believer has been baptized in the
Spirit once for all. The Bible is clear on this. Paul says in I
Corinthians 12:13,

> For by one Spirit are [have] we all [been] baptized into
> one body, whether we be Jews or Gentiles, whether we be
> bond or free; and have all been made to drink into one
> Spirit.

This was a "once for all" experience. No one can be saved
without this experience, for Paul says clearly in Romans 8:9,

> . . . Now if any man have not the Spirit of Christ, he is
> none of his.

What then is this experience which sincere believers talk
about when referring to the baptism of the Spirit *after* they are
saved? It is a *filling* with the Spirit. There can be no question
that many who testify to a receiving of joy, victory, peace and
power at some time during their Christian life after they are
saved, have had a definite experience when they yielded themselves to the will of God, whether accompanied by a tremendous
emotional sense of ecstasy or not. We do not for one moment
doubt their testimony. In many cases something really happened, *but* it was not the baptism *in* the Spirit, instead it was
a *filling with the Spirit.* We repeat again and again, much of
the confusion arises from failure to differentiate between the two.
Once this is realized most of the confusion ends. Of course not
all the testimonies of ecstatic experiences are spiritual. There are
also counterfeit baptisms and fillings, which are merely emotional explosions and psychic imaginations. I am speaking *not*
about these outlandish, fanatical, fantastic, unscriptural emotional deceptions with hallucinations, delusions, dreams, voices
and visions as the result of some physical, mental or emotional
illness. I am speaking of the genuine spiritual experience of
a filling with the Spirit. This may or may not be accompanied
by emotional or physical feelings but the real evidence will be
first of all the fruit of the Spirit — love, joy and peace.

In order to dispel the confusion and misunderstanding concerning the work of the Holy Spirit, especially the baptism and
the filling, we have written these messages on the ministry of

the Holy Spirit. We make no apologies for repeating things we have covered many times previously because the subject demands emphasis and because to many others the old things will be quite new. Once more we want to point out the teaching of the Word concerning the filling *with* the Spirit as differentiated from the baptism. The baptism in the Spirit was once for all, at Pentecost.

However, the filling with the Spirit is an experience which can be repeated whenever the believer meets the conditions. The clearest passage concerning this filling is Ephesians 5:18-20,

> And be not drunk with wine, wherein is excess; but be filled with the Spirit;
> Speaking to yourselves in psalms and hymns and spiritual songs, singing and making melody in your heart to the Lord;
> Giving thanks always for all things unto God and the Father in the name of our Lord Jesus Christ.

Notice first of all how this filling is obtained. It is always passive. It is *be ye filled* — not fill yourselves. It is *be filled* or *allow* yourself to be filled. It cannot be worked up or prayed down. It comes in response to making room for the filling of the Holy Spirit. Nature hates a vacuum and will not tolerate it. If a bottle of water is emptied, air rushes in. To fill a bottle with air, you need not take a pump and start pumping air into the bottle. All this will do is result in a lot of bubbling noise and froth and foam. The simple way to fill the bottle with air is to let the water out, and the air rushes in. So it is with the filling of the Spirit. It will not occupy the same place with sin or a heart filled with worldliness. To be filled with the Spirit means simply emptying your heart of all known and unknown sin, by confession and a complete yielding of your life to God. As long as you tolerate anything in your life which is displeasing to God, the Spirit will not fill you. Examine your heart before God and confess every evil thing; then ask Him to search your heart for things you have overlooked, and say, "Search me, oh God, and know my thoughts." As surely as you do this, you can experience the blessing of being filled with the Spirit. Right now, in full obedience, examine your heart and life; confess all known doubt and disobedience, and as you empty your heart of self the Spirit will take its place. This may or may not be accompanied by great emotional sensation or joy and ecstasy, or it may be only a quiet sense of peace. Now we come to the evidence of being filled with the Spirit. The evidence of the filling of the Holy Spirit is simply given in verse 19 of Ephesians 5,

> Speaking to yourselves in psalms and hymns and spiritual songs, singing and making melody in your heart to the Lord.

No noisy demonstration, no confusion of tongues, no extreme emotional outbursts — but *joy.* The result of the filling of the Spirit is a personal sense of peace and quietness and an inner joy. Notice the wording of Paul. He says the evidence of the filling of the Spirit is "speaking to yourselves in psalms and hymns and spiritual songs." There is no suggestion of loud outbursts or shouting. It is speaking to yourselves, and a singing heart of praise and joy. If a person is really filled with the Spirit he will not have to advertise it by outbursts of ecstasy. People will soon recognize a person really filled with the Spirit by his conduct and godliness. Notice, in addition to speaking to *yourselves,* Paul says that the Spirit is manifested by singing and making melody *in your heart* unto the Lord. To be filled with the Spirit results in a melody, and that melody is not a public display, but is in the heart; it is not for effect upon others, but it is *unto* the Lord. The testimony of a Spirit-filled Christian is called a melody, not a discordant noisemaking or jargon of confusion — but a sweet harmony.

THE NEED

The filling of the Holy Spirit is the greatest need of Christians today. Our churches are full of defeated, starved and seeking believers who know there is more to salvation than just being saved. This sense of the need of a deeper experience, a closer touch with God, can be satisfied by being filled with the Spirit. This accounts for the many who, while seeking such an experience without understanding the Bible requirements, go to all kinds of unscriptural extremes, confusing emotional upsets and physical sensations with true fulness of the Spirit.

However, we must also recognize that among those who testify of an emotional upheaval and a definite experience of so-called baptism with the Spirit, there are many who have really received blessing and joy and victory. In response to earnest seeking, confession of sins, cleansing of heart, they did experience a great feeling of relief, blessing and joy. But the trouble is that these dear people confuse *baptism* and *filling*. We do not deny that there is a blessing, a joy, a victory in yielding to the Spirit (whether accompanied by emotional excitement or not) but this is not a *baptism* in the Spirit; it is rather a *filling with* the Spirit.

Every believer should seek to be filled with the Spirit for greater service and fruitfulness. Is there a hunger in your heart for a deeper life, a greater joy, a closer walk with God? Or to put it simply, Do you desire the fulness of the Holy Spirit? You can have it whenever you meet the conditions of self-examination, honest confession of every known sin, and a complete yielding to God's will. You need not tarry at the altar or "pray through," or go through emotional or physical contortions. If you will make room for Him, He will rush right in.

Examine your heart. Confess to the Lord everything you know is wrong or doubtful. Surrender it to Him and trust Him to keep you. You know what it is that needs to be confessed. Is it some sin, some habit, some secret practice? Is it pride or jealousy or covetousness? Is it a sharp tongue or an uncontrollable temper? Is it gossip, or an unforgiving spirit? Or the sin of criticizing and judging others? Listen, right where you are, tell the Lord about it. Confess that sin to Him. Tell Him you want victory and you are trusting Him to deliver you from that thing which you know is displeasing to God. Confess it, brother, sister, accept His forgiveness and cleansing, and you will experience a filling with the Holy Spirit. This is your great need. Call it baptism, call it second blessing, call it anything you please, but *first get it,* and then recognize it as the *filling* of the Spirit of God. Then if you feel like singing, sing; if you feel like shouting, shout; but be sure you do it only by the prompting of the Holy Spirit.

So in conclusion, recognize that if you are saved, you have been baptized in the Spirit, and you have *all* of Him. That settles your salvation. But now the Spirit wants all of *you*, and this comes by a complete emptying of self and yielding to the will of God. This is Christian victory. This is the abundant life of which Jesus speaks when He says,

> . . . I am come that they might have life [that is the result of being baptized in the Spirit], and that they might have it more abundantly [that is the result of being *filled* with the Spirit] (John 10:10).

The M. R. De Haan Classic Library

M. R. De Haan spoke to millions of listeners each week for some twenty-seven years on the *Radio Bible Class* broadcast. His academic training included a degree from Hope College, a medical degree from the University of Illinois Medical College, and further study at Western Theological Seminary. He was the author of more than twenty books and countless daily devotionals in *Our Daily Bread*, published by RBC Ministries of Grand Rapids, Michigan.

Anyone interested in solid biblical studies for personal growth will find these titles to be rich sources of insight and inspiration.

Adventures in Faith: Studies in the Life of Abraham
ISBN 0-8254-2481-x   192 pp.   paperback

Daniel the Prophet
ISBN 0-8254-2475-5   344 pp.   paperback

Pentecost and After: Studies in the Book of Acts
ISBN 0-8254-2482-8   184 pp.   paperback

Portraits of Christ in Genesis
ISBN 0-8254-2476-3   192 pp.   paperback

The Romance of Redemption: Studies in the Book of Ruth
ISBN 0-8254-2480-1   184 pp.   paperback

Studies in First Corinthians
ISBN 0-8254-2478-x   192 pp.   paperback

Studies in Galatians
ISBN 0-8254-2477-1   192 pp.   paperback

Studies in Hebrews
ISBN 0-8254-2479-8   216 pp.   paperback

Available from Christian bookstores or

kregel
PUBLICATIONS

P.O. Box 2607 • Grand Rapids, MI 49501-2607